Academic

Preparation

In Foreign Language

Teaching for Transition
From High School
To College

College Entrance Examination Board, New York, 1986

Academic Preparation in Foreign Language is one of a series of six books. The Academic Preparation Series includes books in English, the Arts, Mathematics, Science, Social Studies, and Foreign Language. Single copies of any one of these books can be purchased for $6.95. Orders for 5 through 49 copies of a single title receive a 20 percent discount; orders for 50 or more copies receive a 50 percent discount.

A boxed set of all the books in the Academic Preparation Series is available for $20. Orders for five or more sets receive a 20 percent discount. Each set also includes a copy of *Academic Preparation for College: What Students Need to Know and Be Able to Do.*

Payment or purchase order for individual titles or the set should be addressed to: College Board Publications, Box 886, New York, New York 10101.

ISBN: 0-87447-225-3

9 8 7 6 5 4 3 2 1

Contents

Principal Writers and Consultants

Judith E. Liskin-Gasparro, Senior Examiner, Educational Testing Service, Princeton, New Jersey

June K. Phillips, Professor of Foreign Languages and Literatures and Associate Dean, College of Humanities and Social Sciences, Indiana University of Pennsylvania

Foreign Language Advisory Committee, 1984-85

Raul S. Rodriguez, Chairman, Language Department, Xaverian High School, Brooklyn, New York *(Chair)*

Thomas R. Beyer, Jr., Dean, The Russian School, Middlebury College, Vermont

Lucien R. Boisvert, Teacher, Hamden High School, Connecticut

Barbara Crockett Dease, Head and Professor, Department of Modern Foreign Languages, Jackson State University, Mississippi

Vicki B. Galloway, Project Director, American Council of Teachers of Foreign Language, Hastings-on-Hudson, New York

Carmen Salazar, Professor of Spanish, Los Angeles Valley College, California

Maria M. Tatar, Professor of German, Harvard University, Cambridge, Massachusetts

Acknowledgments

The College Board wishes to thank all the individuals and organizations that contributed to *Academic Preparation in Foreign Language*. In addition to those who served on the Foreign Language Advisory Committee and the Council on Academic Affairs, explicit acknowledgment should be accorded to Yola Coffeen, Robert Orrill, Mary Carroll Scott, Hope V. Harris, and Carol J. Meyer. Without the contribution of Glenn M. Knudsvig of the University of Michigan, the support of Frank W. Medley, Jr., of the University of South Carolina, and the leadership of Adrienne Y. Bailey, Vice President for Academic Affairs at the College Board, this book would not have assumed its present form. Although none of these people individually is responsible for the contents of the book, the Educational EQuality Project owes much to their efforts. In working with Diane L. Olsen to bring this book and its five companions to publication, I have incurred my own personal debt.

James Herbert, General Editor

The College Board is a nonprofit membership organization that provides tests and other educational services for students, schools, and colleges. The membership is composed of more than 2,500 colleges, schools, school systems, and education associations. Representatives of the members serve on the Board of Trustees and advisory councils and committees that consider the College Board's programs and participate in the determination of its policies and activities.

The Educational EQuality Project is a 10-year effort of the College Board to strengthen the academic quality of secondary education and to ensure equality of opportunity for postsecondary education for all students. Begun in 1980, the project is under the direction of the Board's Office of Academic Affairs.

For more information about the Educational EQuality Project and inquiries about this report, write to the Office of Academic Affairs, The College Board, 45 Columbus Avenue, New York, New York 10023-6917.

To Our Fellow Teachers of Foreign Language

This book is for our colleagues who teach foreign language. We invite you to join us in an effort to improve foreign language education for all students, particularly at the high school level. Our goal is to change the outcomes of high school language programs so that more students will develop usable skills and realistic cultural awareness.

We have tried to specify the outcomes that we believe should result from the teaching of foreign language and have offered some suggestions for achieving these outcomes. We view our ideas as the beginning of a dialogue, not as a prescription. We have learned from past curriculum reforms that new ideas about teaching are effective only when they can be adapted by individual teachers to fit their own talents, experiences, and particular teaching situations. Moreover, there are many ways in which we can learn from one another to improve language teaching.

In Chapter 1 we locate the book with respect to the entire Educational EQuality Project. Chapter 2 explains the needed outcomes of foreign language study, expanding on the statements of these outcomes in *Academic Preparation for College*. The central concept of proficiency in another language is clarified and developed. Chapter 3 focuses on curriculum, outlining a process that departments and districts can use to move from overall program outcomes to decisions about the content of specific courses. Chapter 4 is devoted to classroom strategies and gives suggestions to implement our goal of proficiency-based teaching. The larger question of the relationship between foreign language study and the development of such Basic Academic Competencies as reading, writing, speaking and listening, reasoning, observing, studying, mathematics, and using computers is the subject of Chapter 5. Chapter 6 looks to the future, raising questions for further discussion.

Several major themes are the foundation of this book. The primary theme is our commitment to foreign language study and our desire to reach more students. Indeed, it is this commitment that has moved us to participate in the Educational EQuality Project and to prepare this book. We recognize that foreign language teachers at all levels—elementary, secondary, and postsecondary—are joined in a common endeavor. By working closely together, we will better serve more students and our profession as well.

A second theme of this book is the interrelationship of language and culture and of foreign language education and multicultural education. Recent dramatic changes in ethnic and linguistic climate have helped us recognize broader horizons. Increasingly, we are coming to recognize that the bilingualism and biculturalism of our fellow citizens are resources to be encouraged and developed, not only in our classrooms but in the nation as a whole.

A final theme is realistic expectations. In most schools foreign language is an elective subject. Students come to us by choice and are often free to stop foreign language study when they wish. Many leave us before they attain a usable level of skill. The typical two-year high school sequence has fewer than 300 hours of actual instruction time. Except in the most unusual circumstances, the outcomes advocated in the Green Book and elaborated in this book cannot be attained in two years. It is our strong conviction that we must give all students the time they really need to develop their language proficiency.

In our classrooms we strive to find new ways to motivate, to interest students whose awareness of the world has not yet gone beyond their immediate environs. We can not, of course, promise instant bilingualism. Students must be told honestly that the payoff is long-range, that just as they have spent years mastering one language, the second one will also require a serious commitment of time and effort. At the same time we must do our part to ensure that opportunities to communicate are provided from the start so that students can begin early to enjoy some of the fruits of their efforts. As language teachers, we also have the responsibility to show students that "foreign" need not mean "odd" or "strange," that cultural diversity is desirable, that while other people's values are sometimes the same as ours and at other times different, similarities and differences are in themselves neither right nor wrong.

By learning a foreign language, a student can enter another world as a person who speaks only one language never can. Beyond our immediate tasks of teaching a given language, we develop in students those skills of communication that help them understand others and share the humanity that is the heritage of us all.

Foreign Language Advisory Committee

I. Beyond the Green Book

*Identifying the academic preparation needed for col-
lege is a first step toward providing that preparation
for all students who might aspire to higher education.
But the real work of actually achieving these learning
outcomes lies ahead.*[1]

This book is a sequel to *Academic Preparation for College: What
Students Need to Know and Be Able to Do,* which was published in
1983 by the College Board's Educational EQuality Project. Now
widely known as the Green Book, *Academic Preparation for College*
outlined the knowledge and skills students need in order to have a
fair chance at succeeding in college. It summarized the combined
judgments of hundreds of educators in every part of the country.
The Green Book sketched learning outcomes that could serve as
goals for high school curricula in six Basic Academic Subjects:
English, the arts, mathematics, science, social studies, and foreign
language. It also identified six Basic Academic Competencies on
which depend, and which are further developed by, work in these
subjects. Those competencies are reading, writing, speaking and
listening, mathematics, reasoning, and studying. The Green Book
also called attention to additional competencies in using computers
and observing, whose value to the college entrant is increasingly
being appreciated.

With this book we take a step beyond *Academic Preparation for
College.* The Green Book simply outlined desired results of high
school education—the learning all students need to be adequately
prepared for college. It contained no specific suggestions about how
to achieve those results. Those of us working with the Educational
EQuality Project strongly believed—and still believe—that ultimately curriculum and instruction are matters of local expertise

---

1. The College Board, *Academic Preparation for College: What Students Need to
Know and Be Able to Do* (New York: College Entrance Examination Board, 1983),
p. 31.

4

and responsibility. Building consensus on goals, while leaving flexible the means to achieve them, makes the most of educators' ability to respond appropriately and creatively to conditions in their own schools. Nevertheless, teachers and administrators, particularly those closely associated with the EQuality project, often have asked how the outcomes sketched in the Green Book might be translated into actual curricula and instructional practices—how they can get on with the "real work" of education. These requests in part seek suggestions about how the Green Book goals might be achieved; perhaps to an even greater extent they express a desire to get a fuller picture of those very briefly stated goals. Educators prefer to think realistically, in terms of courses and lessons. Discussion of proposals such as those in the Green Book proceeds more readily when goals are filled out and cast into the practical language of possible courses of action.

To respond to these requests for greater detail, and to encourage further nationwide discussion about what should be happening in our high school classrooms, teachers working with the Educational EQuality Project have prepared this book and five like it, one in each of the Basic Academic Subjects. By providing suggestions about how the outcomes described in *Academic Preparation for College* might be achieved, we hope to add more color and texture to the sketches in that earlier publication. We do not mean these suggestions to be prescriptive or definitive, but to spark more detailed discussion and ongoing dialogue among our fellow teachers who have the front line responsibility for ensuring that all students are prepared adequately for college. We also intend this book and its companions for guidance counselors, principals, superintendents, and other officials who must understand the work of high school teachers if they are better to support and cooperate with them.

Students at Risk, Nation at Risk

Academic Preparation for College was the result of an extensive grass-roots effort involving hundreds of educators in every part of the country. However, it was not published in a vacuum. Since the beginning of this decade, many blue-ribbon commissions and studies also have focused attention on secondary education. The concerns of these reports have been twofold. One, the reports note a perceptible decline in the academic attainments of students who graduate from high school, as indicated by such means as standardized test scores and comments from employers; two, the reports reflect a widespread worry that, unless students are better educated, our national welfare will be in jeopardy. *A Nation at Risk* made this point quite bluntly:

> Our Nation is at risk. Our once unchallenged preeminence in commerce, industry, science, and technological innovation is being overtaken by competitors throughout the world. . . . The educational foundations of our society are presently being eroded by a rising tide of mediocrity that threatens our very future as a Nation and a people.[2]

The Educational EQuality Project, an effort of the College Board throughout the decade of the 1980s to improve both the quality of preparation for college and the equality of access to it, sees another aspect of risk: if our nation is at risk because of the level of students' educational attainment, then we must be more concerned with those students who have been most at risk.

Overall, the predominance of the young in our society is ending. In 1981, as the EQuality project was getting under way, about 41 percent of our country's population was under 25 years old and 26 percent was 50 years old or older. By the year 2000, however, the balance will have shifted to 34 percent and 28 percent, respectively. But these figures do not tell the whole story, especially for those of us working in the schools. Among certain groups, youth is a growing segment of the population. For example, in 1981, 71 percent of black and 75 percent of Hispanic households had children 18 years old or younger. In comparison, only 52 percent of all white households had children in that age category. At the beginning of the 1980s, children from minority groups already made up more than 25 percent of all public school students.[3] Clearly, concern for im-

---

2. National Commission on Excellence in Education, *A Nation at Risk* (Washington, D.C.: U.S. Government Printing Office, 1983), p. 5.

3. Ernest L. Boyer, *High School* (New York: Harper & Row, 1983), pp. 4-5. U.S. Department of Education, National Center for Education Statistics, *Digest of Education Statistics: 1982* (Washington, D.C.: U.S. Government Printing Office, 1982), p. 43.

proving the educational attainments of all students increasingly must involve concern for students from such groups of historically disadvantaged Americans.

How well will such young people be educated? In a careful and thoughtful study of schools, John Goodlad found that "consistent with the findings of virtually every study that has considered the distribution of poor and minority students . . . minority students were found in disproportionately large percentages in the low track classes of the multiracial samples [of the schools studied]."[4] The teaching and learning that occur in many such courses can be disappointing in comparison with that occurring in other courses. Goodlad reported that in many such courses very little is expected, and very little is attempted.[5]

When such students are at risk, the nation itself is at risk, not only economically but morally. That is why this book and its five companions offer suggestions that will be useful in achieving academic excellence for *all* students. We have attempted to take into account that the resources of some high schools may be limited and that some beginning high school students may not be well prepared. We have tried to identify ways to keep open the option of preparing adequately for college as late as possible in the high school years. These books are intended for work with the broad spectrum of high school students—not just a few students and not only those currently in the "academic track." We are convinced that many more students can—and, in justice, should—profit from higher education and therefore from adequate academic preparation.

Moreover, many more students actually enroll in postsecondary education than currently follow the "academic track" in high school. Further, discussions with employers have emphasized that many of the same academic competencies needed by college-bound students also are needed by high school students going directly into the world of work. Consequently, the Educational EQuality Project, as its name indicates, hopes to contribute to achieving a democratic excellence in our high schools.

---

4. John Goodlad, *A Place Called School* (New York: McGraw-Hill, 1984), p. 156.
5. Ibid., p. 159.

The Classroom: At the Beginning as Well as the End of Improvement

A small book such as this one, intended only to stimulate dialogue about what happens in the classroom, cannot address all the problems of secondary education. On the other hand, we believe that teachers and the actual work of education—that is to say, curriculum and instruction—should be a more prominent part of the nationwide discussion about improving secondary education.

A 1984 report by the Education Commission of the States found that 44 states either had raised high school graduation requirements or had such changes pending. Twenty-seven states had enacted new policies dealing with instructional time, such as new extracurricular policies and reduced class sizes.[6] This activity reflects the momentum for and concern about reform that has been generated recently. It demonstrates a widespread recognition that critiques of education without concrete proposals for change will not serve the cause of improvement. But what will such changes actually mean in the classroom? New course requirements do not necessarily deal with the academic quality of the courses used to fulfill those requirements. Certain other kinds of requirements can force instruction to focus on the rote acquisition of information to the exclusion of fuller intellectual development. Manifestly, juggling of requirements and courses without attention to what needs to occur between teachers and students inside the classroom will not automatically produce better-prepared students. One proponent of reform, Ernest Boyer, has noted that there is danger in the prevalence of "quick-fix" responses to the call for improvement. "The depth of discussion about the curriculum . . . has not led to a serious and creative look at the nature of the curriculum. . . . states [have not asked] what we ought to be teaching."[7]

Such questioning and discussion is overdue. Clearly, many im-

---

6. *Action in the States: Progress toward Education Renewal*, A Report by the Task Force on Education for Economic Growth (Denver, Colorado: Education Commission of the States, 1984), p. 27.

7. In Thomas Toch, "For School Reform's Top Salesmen, It's Been Some Year," *Education Week*, June 6, 1984, p. 33.

provements in secondary education require action outside the classroom and the school. Equally clearly, even this action should be geared to a richer, more developed understanding of what is needed in the classroom. By publishing these books we hope to add balance to the national debate about improving high school education. Our point is not only that it is what happens between teachers and students in the classroom that makes the difference. Our point is also that what teachers and students do in classrooms must be thoughtfully considered before many kinds of changes, even exterior changes, are made in the name of educational improvement.

From Deficit to Development

What we can do in the classroom is limited, of course, by other factors. Students must be there to benefit from what happens in class. Teachers know firsthand that far too many young people of high school age are no longer even enrolled. Nationally, the dropout rate in 1980 among the high school population aged 14 to 34 was 13 percent. It was higher among low-income and minority students. Nearly 1 out of 10 high schools had a dropout rate of over 20 percent.[8]

Even when students stay in high school, we know that they do not always have access to the academic preparation they need. Many do not take enough of the right kinds of courses. In 1980, in almost half of all high schools, a majority of the students in each of those schools was enrolled in the "general" curriculum. Nationwide, only 38 percent of high school seniors had been in an academic program; another 36 percent had been in a general program; and 24 percent had followed a vocational/technical track. Only 39 percent of these seniors had enrolled for three or more years in history or social studies; only 33 percent had taken three or more years of mathematics; barely 22 percent had taken three or more

---

8. National Center for Education Statistics, *Digest of Education Statistics: 1982*, p. 68. Donald A. Rock et al., "Factors Associated with Test Score Decline: Briefing Paper" (Princeton, New Jersey: Educational Testing Service, December 1984), p. 4.

years of science; and less than 8 percent of these students had studied Spanish, French, or German for three or more years.[9]

Better than anyone else, teachers know that, even when students are in high school and are enrolled in the needed academic courses, they must attend class regularly. Yet some school systems report daily absence rates as high as 20 percent. When 1 out of 5 students enrolled in a course is not actually there, it is difficult even to begin carrying out a sustained, coherent program of academic preparation.

As teachers we know that such problems cannot be solved solely by our efforts in the classroom. In a world of disrupted family and community structures; economic hardship; and rising teenage pregnancy, alcoholism, and suicide, it would be foolish to believe that attention to curriculum and instruction can remedy all the problems leading to students' leaving high school, taking the wrong courses, and missing classes. Nonetheless, what happens in the high school classroom—once students are there—is important in preparing students not only for further education but for life.

Moreover, as teachers, we also hope that what happens in the classroom at least can help students stick with their academic work. Students may be increasingly receptive to this view. In 1980 more than 70 percent of high school seniors wanted greater academic emphasis in their schools; this was true of students in all curricula. Mortimer Adler may have described a great opportunity:

> There is little joy in most of the learning they [students] are now compelled to do. Too much of it is make-believe, in which neither teacher nor pupil can take a lively interest. Without some joy in learning—a joy that arises from hard work well done and from the participation of one's mind in a common task—basic schooling cannot initiate the young into the life of learning, let alone give them the skill and the incentive to engage in it further.[10]

Genuine academic work can contribute to student motivation and persistence. Goodlad's study argues strongly that the widespread

9. National Center for Education Statistics, *Digest of Education Statistics: 1982*, p. 70.

10. Mortimer J. Adler, *The Paideia Proposal: An Educational Manifesto* (New York: Macmillan, 1982), p. 32.

focus on the rote mechanics of a subject is a surefire way to distance students from it or to ensure that they do not comprehend all that they are capable of understanding. Students need to be encouraged to become inquiring, involved learners. It is worth trying to find more and better ways to engage them actively in the learning process, to build on their strengths and enthusiasms. Consequently, the approaches suggested in these books try to shift attention from chronicling what students do not know toward developing the full intellectual attainments of which they are capable and which they will need in college.

Dimensions for a Continuing Dialogue

This book and its five companions were prepared during 1984 and 1985 under the aegis of the College Board's Academic Advisory Committees. Although each committee focused on the particular issues facing its subject, the committees had common purposes and common approaches. Those purposes and approaches may help give shape to the discussion that this book and its companions hope to stimulate.

Each committee sought the assistance of distinguished writers and consultants. The committees considered suggestions made in the dialogues that preceded and contributed to *Academic Preparation for College* and called on guest colleagues for further suggestions and insights. Each committee tried to take account of the best available thinking and research but did not merely pass along the results of research or experience. Each deliberated about those findings and then tried to suggest approaches that had actually worked to achieve learning outcomes described in *Academic Preparation for College*. The suggestions in these books are based to a great extent on actual, successful high school programs.

These books focus not only on achieving the outcomes for a particular subject described in the Green Book but also on how study of that subject can develop the Basic Academic Competencies. The learning special to each subject has a central role to play in preparing students for successful work in college. That role ought not to be neglected in a rush to equip students with more general skills. It is learning in a subject that can engage a student's interest, activity, and commitment. Students do, after all, read about *something*, write about *something*, reason about *something*. We thought it important to suggest that developing the Basic Academic Competencies does not replace, but can result from, mastering the unique knowledge and skills of each Basic Academic Subject. Students, particularly hungry and undernourished ones, should not be asked to master the use of the fork, knife, and spoon without being served an appetizing, full, and nourishing meal.

In preparing the book for each subject, we also tried to keep in mind the connections among the Basic Academic Subjects. For example, the teaching of English and the other languages should build on students' natural linguistic appetite and development— and this lesson may apply to the teaching of other subjects as well. The teaching of history with emphasis on the full range of human experience, as approached through both social and global history, bears on the issue of broadening the "canon" of respected works in literature and the arts. The teaching of social studies, like the teaching of science, involves mathematics not only as a tool but as a mode of thought. There is much more to make explicit and to explore in such connections among the Basic Academic Subjects. Teachers may teach in separate departments, but students' thought is probably not divided in the same way.

Finally, the suggestions advanced here generally identify alternative ways of working toward the same outcomes. We wanted very much to avoid any hint that there is one and only one way to achieve the outcomes described in *Academic Preparation for College*. There are many good ways of achieving the desired results, each one good in its own way and in particular circumstances. By describing alternative approaches, we hope to encourage readers of this book to analyze and recombine alternatives and to create the most appropriate and effective approaches, given their own particular situations.

We think that this book and its five companion volumes can be useful to many people. Individual teachers may discover suggestions that will spur their own thought about what might be done in the classroom; small groups of teachers may find the book useful in reconsidering the foreign language program in their high school. It also may provide a takeoff point for in-service sessions. Teachers in several subjects might use it and its companions to explore concerns, such as the Basic Academic Competencies, that range across the high school curriculum. Principals may find these volumes useful in refreshing the knowledge and understanding on which their own instructional leadership is based.

We also hope that these books will prove useful to committees of teachers and officials in local school districts and at the state level who are examining the high school curriculum established in their jurisdictions. Public officials whose decisions directly or indirectly affect the conditions under which teaching and learning occur may find in them an instructive glimpse of the kinds of things that should be made possible in the classroom.

Colleges and universities may find in all six books occasion to consider not only how they are preparing future teachers, but also whether their own curricula will be suited to students receiving the kinds of preparation these books suggest. But our greatest hope is that this book and its companions will be used as reference points for dialogues between high school and college teachers. It was from such dialogues that *Academic Preparation for College* emerged. We believe that further discussions of this sort can provide a wellspring of insight and energy to move beyond the Green Book toward actually providing the knowledge and skills all students need to be successful in college.

We understand the limitations of the suggestions presented here. Concerning what happens in the classroom, many teachers, researchers, and professional associations can speak with far greater depth and detail than is possible in the pages that follow. This book aspires only to get that conversation going, particularly across the boundaries that usually divide those concerned about education, and especially as it concerns the students who often are least well served. Curriculum, teaching, and learning are far too central to be omitted from the discussion about improving education.

II. Preparation and Outcomes

Academic Preparation for College sets forth needed outcomes of high school foreign language study based on the concept of *language proficiency*. What constitutes proficiency in a second, or foreign, language? What are the particular skills and knowledge that should be the outcomes of high school language study? What preparation in a foreign language do students need to pursue advanced language study in college, and what should students bring with them when they begin language study at the high school level?

Proficiency, the Foundation

Mastery of another language has always been the goal of foreign language study. Yet the interpretation of mastery, and the decision about exactly what aspects of language should be emphasized, have changed over the years. Beginning in the nineteenth century and lasting until relatively recently, the unspoken, if not explicit, goal of foreign language study was knowledge of the grammar of the language. This goal, in turn, gave rise to course objectives, methods, and materials that emphasized analysis of grammatical forms, memorization of vocabulary, and translation.

Recently, the grammar-translation approach to language teaching has yielded to new approaches that have in common a focus on students' ability to use the language outside the classroom. This is what *proficiency* means: students emerge from their language programs able, to some degree, to operate in the language as it is written and spoken by native speakers. The concept of proficiency focuses on the *outcomes* of language study, not on methodology. When we speak of a person's proficiency in a language, we mean the ability to understand, read, write, or speak the language compared with that of educated native speakers. The concept is based on what the person can do with the language, independent of how the language was learned, what materials were used, or what methods were involved.

This orientation toward proficiency comes from a desire to make sure that students go on to college with a usable level of skill. If their foundation is solid, they will be able to continue their language studies in college on a more sophisticated level, studying literary texts and cultural documents in that language.

The level of proficiency that we aim for with high school students is different from the level of proficiency that would be the desired outcome of an undergraduate major program. While the term *proficiency* means in both cases the ability to communicate in another language and culture, proficiency has many levels. The question to be asked is always "proficient to do 'what'?" or "able to communicate 'what'?" We want high school students to become proficient enough to survive in another language, to converse on familiar topics, and to work within carefully defined areas. It would be unrealistic, however, to expect them to become proficient enough to read foreign language novels regularly for pleasure or to understand the rhetoric of political speeches.

The outcome statements in the Green Book are consonant with the *ACTFL (American Council on the Teaching of Foreign Languages) Provisional Proficiency Guidelines.*[1] The ACTFL guidelines are a series of paragraph-length descriptions of proficiency in listening, reading, writing, speaking, and culture that span the range from no knowledge of the language to the Superior level, the proficiency that would be needed by an adult working in a professional context. The ACTFL guidelines and the literature that has been written about them are a valuable resource for understanding and expanding on the meaning embedded in the Green Book outcome statements.

Each of the outcome statements can be identified as a statement about function, content, or accuracy. The ACTFL guidelines also can be divided into statements about each of these three elements.

---

1. Copies of the *ACTFL Provisional Proficiency Guidelines* can be obtained at a modest cost from the American Council on the Teaching of Foreign Languages, 579 Broadway, Hastings-on-Hudson, New York 10706.

Function refers to the tasks that learners can perform, such as asking questions or comprehending the gist of a printed or spoken message. *Context* denotes the subjects or topics that learners can understand, or can talk or write about. *Accuracy* involves the precision or correctness with which learners can communicate or comprehend. The Green Book's learning outcomes for all college-bound students correspond to function, context, or accuracy at the Intermediate level of the ACTFL guidelines. The outcomes needed by students who wish to follow an advanced program of language study in college refer to the Advanced level of the ACTFL guidelines.

The Learning Outcomes

The high school years should provide students with the opportunity to develop some reasonable proficiency in each of the four skills of speaking, listening, reading, and writing, as well as occasions for observing the foreign culture and behaving in ways appropriate to it. The proficiency outcomes recommended for foreign language are attainable by the vast majority of high school students if they are provided with the chance to build on sequences of learned material. All students communicate in their native language and can benefit by practicing communicative skills in a new language; it is neither a subject for the elite nor one that demands superior control of the students' first language in order for them to succeed. All students, their parents, and their teachers should aim for and expect the development of foreign language skills that are usable in real-life contexts.

The intent of proficiency statements is to describe what the students can *do* with the foreign language they are studying. These statements do not specify course content in terms of grammar or vocabulary, nor do they say how long the high school foreign language sequence should be. By concentrating on outcomes—the end product—they encourage teachers to design curricula that will reach these objectives. The next section of this chapter will examine the *APC* outcomes in greater detail, treating first the skills that every college entrant will need, and then the additional preparation recommended for students who plan to follow an advanced program of language study in college.

Speaking

- *The ability to ask and answer questions and maintain a simple conversation in areas of immediate need and on very familiar topics.*

This outcome summarizes the speaking objective for all college entrants. Students who attain this outcome will be able to talk about themselves and their lives in short informal conversations.

To "maintain a simple conversation" requires the ability to create with language. By that we mean that students can combine and recombine the words they know in new ways to say things they may never have said before. Even very simple conversation is not just a series of questions and answers, but often consists of comments or observations to which the other person responds. Students who are not yet able to create with language can only answer questions that they have heard before with words or phrases they have memorized.

It is essential that as teachers we heed the "ask questions" portion of the statement so that our students become as adept at seeking information as they are at giving it. Most students get a lot of practice in answering questions posed by teachers. The purpose of many of these questions, however, is not to exchange information but for students to practice grammatical constructions. Students are expected to answer in complete sentences, recycling as much of the language of the questions as possible. When students ask questions, on the other hand, they have to exercise linguistic creativity to open new subject areas and decide what to ask and how to ask it.

What content is expected at this level? What can students talk about? The recommendation suggests areas of "immediate need" and "very familiar topics." Immediate need may include those language functions involved in travel, such as ordering food, obtaining lodging, and getting transportation. It may also include basic social interaction with speakers of other languages, such as greetings, introductions, leave-takings, and other social conventions. Teachers will have to relate the area of very familiar topics to what they know of students' lives, interests, work, and surroundings. This implies providing students with the vocabulary they need to talk about their families, homes, jobs, and leisure-time activities. On the surface, the speaking recommendation initially appears short and direct, but acquiring the skill to carry out these tasks will demand an extensive investment of student and teacher time, practice with many patterns and personalized vocabulary, and exposure to strategies for communication.

The second outcome, which also refers to an aspect of speaking, relates to the degree of accuracy expected of college entrants. It suggests that foreign language students acquire

- *The ability to pronounce the language well enough to be intelligible to native speakers.*

Only two decades ago it was believed that we could train students to have "near-native" pronunciation in a short period of time. Now that we know more about language acquisition, we realize that students who begin language study as adolescents may acquire near-native pronunciation only after years of effort and practice. The Green Book's objective for pronunciation is not only more realistic and attainable than the near-native pronunciation goal, but also represents a significant shift in emphasis. The focus of the outcome statement is on the intelligibility of the message. This is not to say that teachers should stop asking students to practice the exact pronunciation of discrete sounds, but rather points out that while students' pronunciation or intonation in a controlled exercise or drill may approach native standards, it generally breaks down when students are in the heat of conversation, focusing on content rather than form. Rather than interpreting this as carelessness or error, teachers should understand that this phenomenon is a natural one. Standards set for pronunciation drills, when students can focus exclusively on the sounds, can be quite high, while a standard of overall comprehensibility is much more appropriate for conversation, oral presentations, or other activities in which the focus is on content. Similarly, students vary widely in their ability to imitate sounds and intonation patterns. The level of comprehensibility described in this outcome is basic enough to permit even students who find pronunciation difficult to attain it, with practice.

Listening

The desired outcome for the listening skill is

- *The ability to understand, with some repetition, simple questions and statements.*

This may seem to be a minor dimension of understanding language in the real world. Yet, on closer inspection, we can see that the outcome is compatible with what we expect in terms of speaking. In simple conversation it is not unusual to repeat information, and most statements and questions are delivered in fairly simple, straightforward structures. It is also worth remembering that to reach even this level of understanding, students would need to have been exposed to extensive amounts of listening experience both inside and outside the classroom. Even "simple" questions and statements may be hard for students to understand if they contain unfamiliar vocabulary and structures or are spoken with unaccustomed pronunciation and intonation. Since students do not have control over a message they hear, they often require repetition when listening beyond the controlled classroom setting.

Reading

Thus far we have been discussing oral skills. Reading is the first entry into written language. Here the expected outcome is

- *The ability to read and understand the information presented in a simple paragraph.*

Foreign language teachers can benefit from evaluating what reading really means and comparing first-language reading with reading in a foreign language. The outcome statement says "read and understand," which can be restated as "reading for meaning." Students should be able to read to themselves and understand a paragraph whose content is within the range of their experience, just as they would in their first language. Reading is not pronouncing aloud;

good pronouncers may not necessarily have grasped the message of a written passage, but may simply have mastered the correspondence of symbol and sound.

Linguistic and cognitive strategies are an important aspect of the students' ability to read with understanding paragraphs that they have never seen before but that are at a level appropriate to their overall mastery of a foreign language. Indeed, successful reading occurs when language skill and knowing how to read come together.

One key strategy is guessing the meanings of words from the context. Another is to take advantage of the layout of a printed text and any accompanying illustrations, since these will communicate preliminary information about meaning. Cognates also may be more recognizable in printed than in spoken form, and learning to recognize them is another useful reading strategy.

Chapter 2 of the Green Book discusses reading as a Basic Academic Competency necessary for all college entrants and lists various aspects of reading skill that should be the outcome of a secondary school education. Some of these, such as the ability to grasp the main ideas and the supporting details and the ability to use a dictionary, are outcomes of foreign language study as well. The relationship between foreign language study and the development of the Basic Academic Competencies is discussed at length in Chapter 5.

Writing

While students write often in foreign language courses, much of that work consists only of exercises to reinforce material already studied. The Green Book outcome statement addresses writing as composition:

- *The ability to write a short paragraph on a familiar topic.*

As in speaking, what constitutes a "familiar topic" varies with the age and the interests of the student. For almost all students it is safe to assume that they should be able to write about family, daily life at home and at school, and their own outside interests. Their paragraphs will consist mostly of short, discrete sentences, with some attempts at longer, connected ones. Since the students must express themselves at the level of their language proficiency rather than their thoughts, their writing will communicate best when the structures are simple, even repetitious. Although the outcome statement describes a student's spontaneous first-draft effort, teachers should train students to become more self-conscious writers by the use of such strategies as controlled exercises, rewrites, and peer review.

Language in the Culture

The final proficiency outcome binds together language and culture. The previous statements were oriented toward each of the four skills. The content and context for the expected performances were based in the students' own world and experience. Classroom materials, of course, can transport students into other cultures and inform them about other life-styles and contributions to civilization. A rich diversity of cultures may employ the same language. French-speaking cultures are present, for example, in Africa and Canada, as well as in France itself. But learners trying to communicate naturally will talk about themselves and their own lives. The degree to which we ask them to perform beyond their cultural boundaries is described in this outcome:

- *The ability to deal with some everyday situations in the culture such as greetings, leave-takings, buying food, and asking directions.*

Although this outcome mentions some linguistic tasks that students should be able to carry out, it is also related to knowledge of other cultures and to cultural awareness. On the level of language, students are expected to know the basics of interaction in a tourist or a social context. This might be as travelers, when they will need to know how to ask for directions, purchase bus tickets, or order a meal in a restaurant. Knowledge of numbers and certain formulaic expressions ("Excuse me . . . ," "I would like . . . ," "Can you please tell me . . . ") is particularly useful in these situations. While we recognize that people can survive in another culture without knowing the language, our objective is that foreign language students learn to participate, at least to a limited degree, in the cultures they visit.

Increasingly in our own multicultural society, students will have opportunities to use a foreign language in their own localities. Both at home and abroad, the linguistic skills that students need to communicate with speakers of other languages must be accompanied by knowledge about the culture. For example, students need to know not only what words to use in greetings but also how to vary the greeting according to the time of day, the social context, the age of the individual, and so forth, as well as what gestures to use, such as shaking hands or bowing.

Many students may never travel outside the United States. The culture outcome is still important for all students, because virtually everyone will encounter members of other cultural groups in social or work situations during their adult lives. The awareness of cultural diversity that students gain in the language classroom can assist them in interacting appropriately and more openly with individuals whose customs and language are different from their own. For students whose own ethnic heritage is strongly felt in their lives, the awareness of cultural diversity can help them understand better the experiences of their parents and grandparents in a new land, and see themselves more clearly as heirs to more than one cultural tradition.

Outcomes for Advanced Students

Proficiency in and knowledge of a foreign language develop over a long period of time. Students do not suddenly find themselves "fluent" or "bilingual." Because these skills develop slowly, the proposed learning outcomes for all college entrants are at a very basic, but usable, level. Foreign language learners who stop at this point have taken only the first steps toward lasting enjoyment of and proficiency in a language. If they do not maintain or improve their skills, they probably will lose them and join the group of former language learners who complain, "I took X years of Spanish (or French or Italian) in high school, but I can't say a thing!" The basic outcomes, therefore, should be seen as a first and necessary step toward achieving active, permanent language proficiency. The outcomes for advanced students represent the degree of language proficiency we believe should be expected of all college-educated adults. A small percentage of students will begin language study early enough and embrace it enthusiastically enough to reach this goal before they enter college. These students will begin to be able to think in the language, will communicate with more confidence, and will be able to use the language well enough to gain new knowledge through it.

The outcome statements for advanced students are consonant with the Advanced level proficiency descriptions in the *ACTFL Provisional Proficiency Guidelines*. As with the basic outcomes, each statement deals with an element of the function, context, or accuracy involved in the comprehension or the production of a foreign language.

Advanced students will have further developed their speaking skills so that they demonstrate

- *The ability to engage in conversation about such subjects as school activities, personal interests, and autobiographical information.*

Such students have made gains in both the quality and the quantity of the language they produce. Note "engage in conversation" here compared with "maintain a simple conversation" in the basic outcome for speaking. Advanced students can be involved in a conversation; they talk about a variety of subjects and share information or perceptions in more detail. Their pronunciation and intonation are now good enough for them to be understood by native speakers *not* used to dealing with foreigners. They will often qualify statements and describe things more fully. For example, in talking about personal interests, the basic student might say, "I like music," and then will need a question to cue each additional piece of information. The advanced speaker can expand: "I like music, especially classical. I play the violin and a little piano. I play in the orchestra. There's a concert next week. . . ." With advanced speakers, the language has become a tool for communication.

To develop advanced listening skill, students will need greater opportunities to hear the foreign language. This outcome is stated as

- *The ability to understand the essential points of a lecture, a narrative, or an explanation delivered at moderate speed.*

Students can now meaningfully handle much larger amounts of information in the foreign language. When listening, they are not confused by occasional unfamiliar words or uncommon structures. By keeping the context in mind, they are able to follow the message. As teachers explain or discuss a topic, students can monitor their own understanding and request clarification if needed. Recorded materials coordinated with programs of study provide important listening practice, for the advanced student should comprehend main ideas in this medium as well.

It is perhaps in the realm of reading that advanced students demonstrate the greatest proficiency. They are expected to have acquired

- *The ability to read and comprehend some literature and most factual information in nontechnical prose such as newspaper articles addressed to the general reader.*

Comprehension of literature will vary a great deal from student to student. At the level described by the outcome statement, it is not enough to comprehend the words of a foreign language text. Students may also be asked to describe and analyze the themes, the relationships of characters to each other, and the role of the author or narrator. These skills of analysis, which allow students to read and appreciate literature, are often developed in English classes before students reach the requisite reading proficiency in a foreign language. The same skills of interpretive reading used in English can be applied in the foreign language, once the students are able to read literature in that language. Students who do not have the experience of reading in breadth and depth in their native language, or who do not yet deal well with abstract concepts, will not read literature in a foreign language with the same understanding as do other students. Even so, students at the level of this outcome will be able to read literary or nonliterary prose for factual information.

So it is with newspaper and magazine articles. The ability of students to read news articles in the foreign language is related not only to their proficiency in the language but also to their knowledge of the subject matter and their reading comprehension in general. For example, a high school student who reads the local newspaper may rarely turn to the financial section. Even articles on world events or domestic issues may be read selectively, according to personal or possibly a school interest. Our expectation for reading in a foreign language respects this situation. The "general reader" referred to in the outcome statement is not a specialized or an erudite audience, but rather represents a cross section of society.

As with most of the skills, students at the advanced level will be able to produce writing of greater quality and quantity. Students will develop

- *The ability to write several paragraphs of reasonably coherent and correct prose to produce summaries, descriptions of events, or social correspondence.*

Students at this level find that their mastery of the language now permits them to express their thoughts more precisely. When writing summaries, students probably produce their most linguistically sophisticated product. Such paragraphs are usually based on material recently studied, and the vocabulary and style of that material can serve as a model. More creative assignments require greater recall of words and structures. Consequently, there is more room for error. Students can, however, develop a narrative or a description quite consistently at this level; they can "tell a story" so that the facts of the event, the relevant background, and their reaction to it are communicated. In social correspondence students carry out functions such as extending, accepting, or rejecting invitations; sharing interests; and describing their environment and activities. They should also be able to give and ask for information in either a social letter or an informal business letter.

Finally, the culture outcome anticipates that what the student has learned or observed about living patterns in another society can be integrated into appropriate modes of behavior. It involves

- *The ability to handle routine social situations in a culturally correct manner showing understanding of common rules of how individuals behave toward one another.*

When students know only a few words in a language, it is easy to forgive their errors of social conduct. As their facility with the language grows, however, they will be expected to behave in a more culturally acceptable way. For the commonly taught languages, this means that students might be expected to shake hands, use informal and formal means of address, avoid gestures objectionable in the culture in question, know where and when to tip or not to tip, use correct table manners, and the like. The appropriate form of such practices can vary even among cultures that employ the same language.

25

Taken together, the skill and behavioral outcomes expected of advanced learners imply that these students possess proficiency to a degree that they can actually do a job with that language or use the language to learn subject matter in other fields. Language has become a tool for them, a key with which they can enter domains such as the literature, history, geography, politics, art, or religion of the foreign culture. Their foreign language study may already have advanced their academic knowledge in some of these areas.

Outcomes for Classical Languages

Latin and ancient Greek generally are taught as literary rather than spoken languages. Therefore, the two principal outcomes are reading skills and knowledge of Roman and Greek culture. The expected outcomes in the area of reading are:

- *The ability to read and understand materials of low difficulty—that is, adapted or simplified texts.*
- *The ability to give a reasonably accurate account of the contents of the reading material by answering questions, paraphrasing, translating, or summarizing.*

Reading Latin for understanding is the more difficult of the two outcomes to describe. Since Latin is a language in which most learners are not asked to function as they are in the case of a modern language, Latin students, therefore, do not acquire the reinforcing skills of listening, speaking, and writing to the same level that modern language students do. Hence, the ability to read for understanding at the basic level is characterized by learners' being able to process the words on the printed page in such a way that they acquire specific information about the meaning of the sentence or passage. Achieving the outcome requires that students learn to respond to the morphologic, syntactic, and semantic information carried by each word or group of words. In this way, they begin to grasp how the Latin language worked, and that it was meant to be read, heard, and understood in the form in which we find it today.

Students must be trained and encouraged to consider a passage as a source of information, not just as a collection of words to be pronounced or translated without comprehension. Many methods and techniques are available to help students learn to read for meaning. In addition to those that focus on teaching students to process morphologic, syntactic, and semantic information, there are useful techniques used in first-language learning at all levels. These include such things as surveying a passage and then generating questions to answer while reading, or reading to answer preset questions.

In many classrooms the second outcome is used as the measure of the first; that is, the students' level of understanding of a passage is measured by their abilities in answering questions, paraphrasing, translating, summarizing, and so on. These abilities have a higher status as an outcome for Latin than for modern languages, where one does not need to rely on English as the language for dealing with a passage. The value of separating the two outcomes is that it reminds teachers to analyze each target outcome separately in order to identify the subskills that are required for proficiency in each one.

Learning to answer questions, paraphrase, translate, and summarize demands special training beyond that of learning the Latin language. There are many kinds of questions that learners must be trained to answer. They begin with simple substitution questions in which the structure of the question parallels that of the text. These are the easiest to answer. More effort is required in learning to respond, to transformation questions, in which the structure of the question and of the text are not parallel. Likewise, paraphrasing, translating, and summarizing each demand special training. It is important to note that the ability to analyze and describe the Latin text does not guarantee that one can translate even at a simple or literal level.

Outcomes for Advanced Students

Students who undertake advanced study in a classical language need to develop a higher level of proficiency in the skills described in the basic outcomes. Specifically, these outcomes are:

- *The ability to understand authentic unsimplified prose without undue reliance on a dictionary.*
- *The ability to translate prose or poetry into reasonably accurate English.*

27

It is generally agreed that the ability to understand a Latin text will vary considerably, depending on the difficulty of the text and the students' familiarity with the content. Nevertheless, the information about the language and literature, the rules, and the exercises should all reinforce the movement toward this goal.

The building of translation skills begun at the basic level must continue at this level. This is not only a task of learning more about Latin but also of learning about the different possibilities that exist in English for expressing a particular structure. For example, in what different ways can a past participle that has its own modifiers be expressed, and what are the implications of each possibility?

At this advanced level students will show increased evidence of being able to react to rhetorical devices, the range of possible meanings of words and phrases, semantic compatibility in the use of language, and periodic style. Among the skills students must have are effective dictionary use, a greater awareness of possible semantic categories and features of words, and the ability to translate, when appropriate, long Latin periods into a series of independent English sentences while retaining as much of the impact of the original Latin as possible.

The Starting Point: What Students Bring to Foreign Language Study

What knowledge do students already have that helps them when they begin to study a foreign language? If teachers know what their students bring to foreign language study, they are better able to build on that knowledge so that progress toward the goal of basic proficiency can be made from the beginning.

First and most important, students bring a native language in which they already communicate effectively. Also, being able to read and write in one language means that students have already developed a major cognitive ability. This ability means that the second language can be learned in a way very different from that used in the first language. Teachers can also find ways to develop strong oral skills by using the visual cues and explanations that students have come to employ.

Some students also come to foreign language study with the

ability to analyze and describe the structures and syntax of their own language. Students who have studied the grammar of their own language are able to understand grammatical concepts in the second language relatively easily. Other students have not had this preparation and so will lack formal knowledge of structure. Students who lack strength in this area should not be steered away from foreign language classes. Language can be learned in a more inductive manner; rule generalization can be taught without basing it on another system. Insights gained more consciously through a second language may clarify for the student how the grammar of the native language operates.

Students also bring curiosity and enthusiasm to foreign language study. They not only choose to study a language; in many schools they may select the language as well. Foreign language is usually one of the few new areas for study. Most subjects seem to be continuations: more history, more mathematics, more English. The foreign language teacher offers something new—and a new chance for success as well.

For years we have been advocating foreign language for everyone. If our wish comes true—and there is evidence that foreign language is attracting a broader spectrum of students—teachers must be prepared to teach those who have heard the message. They will have to be responsive to different types of learners and to students with various levels of general preparation. Teaching strategies and methodologies must reflect the fact that students can communicate and are literate in at least one language and already possess many cognitive skills.

Academic Preparation for High School

Learning a foreign language to a useful level of proficiency requires *time* above all else. Ideally, the outcomes for college entrants would be outcomes for high school entrants. Language study would begin in the elementary grades, along with arithmetic, science, social studies, and the like. When Americans marvel at the fluency in English displayed by visitors from abroad, they usually discover that these individuals began their foreign language study during the elementary school years, at or before the age of 10. The best

29

preparation for high school language study, then, is language study in elementary and junior high schools.

Programs scattered throughout this country are experimenting with early foreign language study and foreign language immersion. A few bilingual and foreign language academies have established reputations for excellence. Most of these programs are still considered experimental, but as more research studies come to light and the professional literature elaborates on them, we will see where their strengths lie.

Which of the basic outcomes are best suited for language programs for younger learners? Certainly pronunciation should be emphasized. A wealth of research attests to the fact that preadolescents naturally and easily attain more nativelike pronunciation. Second, these students can progress relatively rapidly to simple conversation. They can acquire a great deal of basic vocabulary in the foreign language, and they are less inhibited about pronouncing unfamiliar sounds than are older students. The "childish" activities and language they are learning are not so distant from their own experiences and therefore are generally not embarrassing to them. In addition, their curiosity leads them to identify and learn the personalized vocabulary necessary to talk about their lives and interests. Younger learners will do less with syntax but can be taught to use a limited number of structures as supports for a more extensive vocabulary. In some of the new immersion and bilingual programs, students develop sophisticated listening skills, especially in programs where content is taught in the foreign language.

No language program that continues as students move from one level of schooling to the next can be completely successful unless teachers work together to coordinate their efforts. This is true for students entering high school as well as for students who go from high school to college. If teachers work together, using a common set of outcomes as their goal, they can then help students progress by building on already acquired skills.

What is the best preparation for foreign language study in high school for students who do not have the opportunity to begin language study earlier in their schooling? To answer this question, we must turn to the Basic Academic Competencies: reading, writing, speaking and listening, mathematics, reasoning, studying, using computers, and observing. Chapter 5 of this book discusses in some depth the relationship of foreign language study to the Basic Academic Competencies. Students who have learned to appreciate language in general, through reading, through writing in different styles and for different audiences, through enjoying the lyrics and cadences of vocal music, will have ears and eyes more attuned to a foreign language. Students who have learned to reason analytically, perhaps through courses in mathematics or knowledge of computers, will bring to foreign language study a sense of language as a self-contained system. Certainly, students who have developed the competencies of studying, speaking, and listening will have skills of concentration and attention that will serve them well in any new academic endeavor.

Finally, students who have grown up in a family or in a school environment in which a language other than English is spoken will have an extra advantage when they come to the formal study of a foreign language. The experience of persons who know several languages often is that the first foreign language was the hardest to learn and that the others came much more easily. Students who are already bilingual will discover that they already know a great deal about language and language learning.

Students who know only one language but who have known speakers of other languages in their neighborhoods and schools also have experienced language in action in a way that youngsters in an English-only environment may not understand. Students who have friends or family members who are speakers of another language can see the usefulness, and the special pleasure, of learning a language in order to communicate with its speakers. They may also appreciate, even if they cannot express it, that each language is a fully functioning system all its own, and that people who produce these unfamiliar sounds are communicating with each other in just as meaningful and valid a way as do speakers of English.

Planning to Achieve the Outcomes

To achieve the outcomes described in this chapter the syllabi for many foreign language courses will need to be restructured. Some aspects of language study should receive greater attention and others should be de-emphasized; the order of presentation may have to be changed. The time devoted to foreign language study may need to be increased so that students are able to acquire the necessary skills and knowledge. A fuller discussion of such curricular issues is presented in Chapter 3.

We have purposely *not* said how many years students should study a foreign language, because we have focused our attention on the outcomes of high school language study. Each school or school district will have to assess the strengths and potential of its own program to decide how best to help more students attain and perhaps move beyond the outcomes described above.

Arrangements should be made whenever possible to enable and encourage all students interested in postsecondary education to continue their study of a foreign language through the last year of high school. Students who have a gap of one year or more in their language study, even if they have reached the basic outcomes, are likely to forget a great deal of what they have learned. They will probably have to repeat material they have already studied.

Foreign language teachers should make special efforts to encourage a wider range of students to pursue the study of a foreign language. If students already speak at home a language that is offered in their schools, they should be encouraged to study that language. They may bring to it knowledge and skills far beyond those of their peers who have studied the language exclusively in a school setting. Special programs or supplementary materials can capitalize on their strengths in oral communication while developing their literacy skills.

The practice of discouraging students with less-developed skills in standard English from enrolling in foreign language classes must also change. Foreign language instruction can be a fresh start for all students and an opportunity for them to start off on an approximately equal footing. The success of some urban schools that emphasize foreign languages is a strong indication that "at risk" students can succeed in language study.

Conclusion

Foreign language study is both intimately connected to the Basic Academic Competencies and a unique subject in its own right.

Students who achieve the basic outcomes described in this chapter will have attained a modest but usable level of proficiency. If they continue to develop their proficiency, they can look forward to using the language for work and pleasure throughout their adult lives.

The structure of the high school foreign language program is a key element in leading students to the outcomes. Chapter 3 treats the topic of the curriculum: how to move from the stated outcomes to the course goals and objectives to the day-to-day teaching that is the heart of students' foreign language learning experience.

III. The Curriculum

After the needed outcomes of foreign language study have been clarified, the next step is to develop a curriculum that will enable students to attain those outcomes. This chapter describes a process by which a proficiency-based, outcome-oriented curriculum can be developed from broad goals to measurable objectives to course outlines and strategies for implementation. We have purposely avoided prescribing or even recommending a particular curriculum, since each school district's needs and resources must be taken into account as it designs its foreign language program. We do recommend that teachers seriously consider and discuss the procedure outlined in this chapter when they next undertake curriculum revision. By answering the questions posed here, teachers and administrators may have a clearer picture of the purpose of their foreign language program—what it aims to do for students and how it intends to accomplish those aims.

What Is a Curriculum?

The structure and much of the content of these observations about curriculum have been inspired by a chapter by Frank W. Medley, Jr., in the 1985 Northeast Conference reports.[1] He begins by reviewing various definitions of the term *curriculum*. For the purposes of this chapter, we have defined it as a set of language-specific goals and course-level objectives. These are used as outcomes around which teachers plan their syllabi (that is, course outlines, lesson plans) and organize their teaching strategies.

Why is a curriculum necessary? Medley makes an analogy between a curriculum and an architect's blueprint. Just as a blueprint

---

1. Frank W. Medley, Jr., "Designing the Proficiency-Based Curriculum," in *Proficiency, Curriculum, Articulation: The Ties That Bind*, ed. Alice C. Omaggio (Middlebury, Vermont: Northeast Conference, 1985), pp. 13–39.

represents a family's decision about the purpose of a home, the needs it should serve, and the features it will contain, so a school district's curriculum depicts in schematic form the result of much careful thinking about the purpose of a language program, realistic expectations, resources, and so forth. A curriculum provides for instruction with purpose, since it clearly states what the goals of a course of study will be.

A curriculum that specifies goals enables teachers to make decisions about how to reach those goals. In addition, a curriculum is a public document that serves not only teachers but also students, parents, and administrators by providing realistic expectations for language study. Finally, a curriculum is necessary to provide level-by-level articulation. Entry and exit performance expectations should be worked out in common by all teachers who teach a particular language in a school or district, so that students will progress smoothly through the program without unnecessary repetition or gaps in content.

This definition of, and rationale for, curriculum have several implications that are worth noting.

1. Given the nature and the history of education in the United States, there will never be a national curriculum in foreign language, nor would it be desirable to have one. Curriculum development is envisioned in this chapter as a process, and each school or district that undertakes this process will have its own special mix of priorities, resources, challenges, and personalities that will affect the curriculum that emerges.

2. Curriculum is most directly understood as what students can do and at what point in the program they can be expected to do it. Questions concerning what the teacher provides to help students grasp the material and arrive at the specified goals are not, strictly speaking, issues of curriculum. Once goals and objectives have been established and courses outlined that will lead students to them, instructional elements can find their rightful place. These include such things as classroom strategies, materials, use of the textbook, and achievement testing.

3. Curriculum design in its pure form is textbook-free. Unfortunately, there is a tradition in education of equating the curriculum with the textbook; the process of curriculum writing then

consists of dividing the table of contents of the textbook into chronological units and considering them the curricular core. This traditional procedure implies, of course, that when there is a change of text, the curriculum has to be rewritten. In addition, the textbook publishers, not the teachers, end up determining the scope and sequence of courses in a program for students and teachers whose particular needs and desires are unknown to them. Teachers, in turn, are involved in the process only indirectly in their choice of textbooks and in their creation of add-ons to the textbook-based curricular core.

In this chapter we advocate that teachers consider the creation of a *proficiency-based curriculum*. By this we mean a curriculum whose goals are related to the *use* of the language in real-life contexts. Functional ability in the language is placed at the center of the curriculum, rather than the mastery of language forms that has so often been the focus of instruction. The proficiency-based curriculum integrates the language functions (tasks to be accomplished in the language), context (thematic domains), and linguistic forms (morphology, syntax, pronunciation) so that successive mastery of each element is dependent on, and contributes to, mastery of the others.

Steps in Curriculum Design

No department in a school can consider itself isolated from the other subject areas or from the school or district as a whole. Everybody—teachers, administrators, students, and parents—is involved in the educational enterprise. Therefore, it makes sense to look at the school's or district's broad statement of educational philosophy and goals. Curriculum guides written by teachers in other subjects may also be helpful. Colleagues in another field may have insights in the area of curriculum development that can be shared with the language teachers. Certainly, from a philosophical as well as a political point of view, the case for support from the administration to design and implement a new or substantially revised curriculum will be strengthened if the language department shows that it is working in harmony with the district's overall educational philosophy, or that language teachers are collaborating with teachers in other departments.

Having completed this preliminary step of finding out more about how the foreign language program fits into the larger context of the school and the district, language teachers can begin to develop their curriculum. The steps outlined by Medley (1985), which we will discuss here, are (1) setting goals, (2) identifying objectives, (3) incorporating the text, and (4) implementing the curriculum.

Step 1: Setting the Goals

Goals are general statements about what students will derive from their study of the language. To organize a language program effectively, goals should be developed in each skill for each yearlong (or, in some cases, semesterlong) course so that the progression can clearly be seen.

It is important to make sure that the goals are realistic. They are not statements about what students should be able to do or what others would like students to do, but about what students *will* be able to do. Consequently, there must be a clear progression of goals from one course to the next, so that the goals and their sequence are easily understandable by students, parents, and administrators. The goals should include broad statements about the linguistic tasks or functions that students will be able to carry out and the contexts in which the functions will be performed. Accuracy requirements at this stage will be described in general terms. For example, for the productive skills, a goal might be that students' language be comprehensible to native speakers; for the receptive skills, the goal might be that students understand certain types of spoken language with some slowing or repetition.

When teachers begin the process of setting goals for each course, they can start either with the first year and work their way up, or with the last year and work their way back. There are dangers in both methods. Starting with the first year may seem to lend itself to the development of more realistic goals, since it is possible to check along the way that students are actually meeting the expectations that have been set. The danger lies in falling into the old pattern of teaching what can be fit into the time available, rather than selecting topics, ordering them, and organizing instruction so that it is oriented at all times toward the goals.

The attraction of starting with the last course and working back to the first-year course is that the contribution of each course to the overall program may be seen more clearly. The danger, however, is that the overall goals are often set unrealistically high, and too much material then has to be packed into the beginning levels.

We hope that the Green Book and the discussion of the outcomes in Chapter 2 of this book will assist teachers in setting overall program goals that are realistic and attainable. Once such goals are drafted, they have to be validated by observation of students and discussion among colleagues. One can then start with either the first or last course in the sequence, developing interim goals and analyzing the components of each course and the progression from one course to another.

Once the goals for each course have been drafted, teachers should ask themselves several questions: How does this compare to what I already do? Is this better than what we do now? Can it be done if the new goals are judged to be both desirable and reasonable? Having answered these questions teachers can then begin the process of deciding what to teach, what to delete, and how to order the course content in order to reach the goals.

It is at the goal-setting stage that the Green Book outcomes fit in. As we explained in Chapter 2, the Green Book outcomes are closely related to the *ACTFL Provisional Proficiency Guidelines,* a valuable resource for teachers who are formulating overall program goals. There are several reasons, however, why the ACTFL guidelines cannot be adopted wholesale as goals for a foreign language program. First, they are widely spaced and cover a range of proficiency levels that is beyond the reach of any secondary school language program. Because of the wide spacing, even at the lower end of the scale there is no obvious progression from one level to the next. Second, the guidelines were written for testing purposes, not for teaching. Consequently, in the ranges of the scale that are likely to be the focus of academic language instruction (that is, Novice and Intermediate), there are more negative ("can't do") than positive statements. Goals must be stated positively to serve as outcomes for instruction.

The Green Book outcomes are also quite general and are meant to serve as overall guidelines in efforts to establish course content and learner performance criteria for one year of study (or two years, three years, and so forth). By developing these Green Book outcome statements at basic and advanced levels, we wish to emphasize that language programs should be designed so that all students can attain at least the basic goals. It is our hope that schools will aim beyond these basic outcomes toward advanced language courses in college so that students can use the language for pleasure and profit in a variety of academic, professional, and recreational settings.

It should be noted that we have purposely not linked these outcome statements to any specific time frame. The number of years needed to achieve the stated levels of performance will vary from one district to another and will depend on many factors, such as class size, student motivation, and teacher preparation.

Step 2: Moving from Goals to Objectives

The goals that serve as the organizing principles for each course are general statements that describe the range of tasks and contexts that students will be able to handle by the end of the year. To make them more specific, they must be broken down into measurable criteria, that is, into *objectives*. It is at the stage of identifying objectives, or way stations in our path toward the course goals, that the various components of language must be balanced so that each element contributes appropriately to the overall goals. This is also the stage at which the curriculum moves from an overall level of expectation to specific performances that will lead to the fulfillment and measurement of goals. Objectives must be concrete, measurable, and practical. If the objectives for a particular course are not reasonable for students with that amount of contact with the language, for example, then no amount of creative implementation will help. Alternatively, if attainment of an objective cannot be measured in some way, the chances are great that the objective will simply be ignored.

Let us look at an example of how a broad goal can be spelled out as a group of measurable objectives. The Green Book outcome statement for speaking is the following: "The ability to ask and answer questions and maintain a simple conversation in areas of immediate need and on very familiar topics." As it stands, the statement is too broad to serve as a springboard for instruction.

Asking and answering questions and maintaining conversations are wide categories that involve many different purposes for communication. The process of developing objectives from a statement such as this involves spelling out specific communicative purposes. These purposes, which can also be expressed as the "immediate need" areas mentioned in the outcome statement, might include such things as meeting people, greeting people, expressing pleasure and displeasure, expressing appreciation, requesting services, asking permission, identifying something or someone, and offering to do something. The list of purposes can be generated from student surveys, teachers' experience of what students want to be able to say, teachers' knowledge of what students will need to do when they talk to speakers of the language, and so on.

After a list of communicative purposes has been drawn up, the next step is to combine them with content areas and cultural contexts. In what contexts (social interaction, making a purchase, helping a stranger) and about what topics will students communicate? The answers to this question constitute the list of objectives. From the speaking goal given above, the following partial list of objectives might be derived:

- Can ask for directions from one place to another
- Can introduce two people to each other in a way that is socially acceptable to native speakers of the language
- Can respond with appropriate verbal formulas and gestures when being introduced to someone
- Can order a meal in a restaurant
- Can appropriately accept or decline offers of food by a host
- Can make purchases; can negotiate price in a situation in which it is appropriate to do so
- Can elicit basic autobiographical information from a person, such as names and occupations of family members, interests, school subjects
- Can give basic autobiographical information, such as names and occupations of family members, interests, school subjects

Each of these objectives involves certain vocabulary domains, grammatical structures, syntactic forms, and sociolinguistic behaviors. By examining carefully the overall goals for each course, the curriculum designers can create a complete list of objectives for listening, reading, writing, speaking, and culture.

Step 3: From Objectives to Implementation: Using the Textbook and Other Materials

Up to this point the curriculum development effort can and should take place without reference to the table of contents of the textbook. Once a group of teachers has established goals and objectives as particular ways in which students will be able to use the language, the next step is to develop a specific day-to-day plan.

The primary resource at the teacher's disposal for this step is the textbook. Considered at this point, after the goals and objectives have been set, the textbook can and should be seen as the servant of the curriculum. Fitting together the objectives and the textbook involves seeing the ways in which the text materials advance students toward the objectives. Most texts are organized so that the theme of each chapter (At School, In the Airport, A Visit to the Museum, In the Doctor's Office) introduces new vocabulary while at the same time providing a context for the presentation of the grammatical topics that are the heart of the chapter. Teachers who have set goals and objectives in terms of functional language use will find that they have to provide the links between the chapter themes and the functional objectives. This process might involve, for example, weaving the function of asking questions into some or all of the chapter themes listed above. In the At School chapter, the curriculum designer would include the function of asking questions by having students ask what time courses meet, what science courses are offered, which courses are the hardest, and so on. A Visit to the Museum is a likely place to include questions about directions (where certain exhibits are located, where the snack bar is, what floor the gift shop is on); about time (hours of operation); about the preferences of their classmates (painting versus drawing, modern versus classical).

The principle illustrated here is one of recycling or spiraling the functions and the content areas. Instead of linking a given function to a single context, we combine and recombine function and context in a variety of ways. This gives students practice in using language flexibly and creatively, applying what they have learned to a variety of linguistic situations.

The principle of spiraling also applies to the presentation and practice of grammar points. Almost all textbooks contain far more grammar than is necessary to lead students to functional objectives. How can teachers decide which grammar topics to introduce and when, and which to postpone or leave out altogether? Ideally, the performance objectives should guide teachers in the selection of the grammar to be taught, with the first priority being to teach the grammar needed to support the functions. For example, in reference to the partial list of speaking objectives on page 40, the following grammatical items are the most important:

- Formation of information questions (where? who? what? how many?)
- Simple subject-verb-object statements involving the verbs to have, to be, to like/want
- Language-specific grammar points dealing with such topics as formation of numbers, irregular verbs or verbal constructions (for example, "to like" in Spanish)

Many of the decisions that follow will be language-specific as teachers reorder the sequence in which grammar is presented. Teachers may want to use some of the following guidelines in deciding what grammar points to retain or emphasize.[2]

- Degree of regularity in formation and use
- Degree of simplicity or complexity
- Frequency of use in real life
- Number of real-life functions to which the structure contributes
- Degree of student interest
- Degree of transferability to other contexts
- Degree of use across all four skills

---

2. The criteria that follow were developed by Vicki B. Galloway for the ACTFL/ University of South Carolina Curriculum Development Workshop, August 1984.

- Degree of native speaker's irritation with misuse
- Versatility/flexibility

This is a time-consuming process, to be sure, but the end result is course organization that incorporates the concept of proficiency and is based on functional objectives. At the same time, moreover, it makes flexible use of a particular text series.

Step 4: Implementation

With the blueprint in place, teachers are ready to think about the teaching methods and the day-to-day classroom activities that will bring students and course content together. We have suggested some ways to approach classroom activities in Chapter 4. Teachers should periodically match student performance against the objectives, in order to assess whether the objectives are realistic and if adjustments are necessary. Ideally, the process of curriculum development is as ongoing and as organic as the language itself.

The Place of Culture in the Curriculum

Today, more than ever before, culture and language exist side by side in the foreign language curriculum. Textbooks take great care to present authentic visual and written cultural materials. The type of cultural information sometimes referred to as "capital *C*," or civilization, still receives coverage, but it has taken second place to the "small *c*" culture, that is, the life-style and customs of a people. The curriculum should make room to accommodate both.

Once language outcomes are stated in proficiency terms, the decision to integrate cultural concepts throughout the program must follow. Language without culture serves no meaningful communicative purpose. From Lesson One of the beginning course, students should be made aware that even basic greetings and leave-takings involve more than translations from English. They must also pay attention to (1) accompanying gestures, such as shaking hands or bowing; (2) proper forms of address and names; and (3) a range of courtesy formulas. Such sociolinguistic patterns should be emphasized in the curriculum and throughout each course of study.

If we return once again to the list of speaking objectives on page 40, we can see the importance of cultural elements throughout. For example, for students to "introduce two people to each other in a way that is socially acceptable to native speakers," they will have to know such things as whose name to give first, whether to use formal or familiar address, whether it is necessary or desirable to say something about each person and, if so, what to say. Similarly, to ask directions of someone on the street, it is important to know how to attract the person's attention and how to respond to the information.

The overall goals for culture in a foreign language program can be divided into two types. The first is information about the culture, whether that be knowledge about geographical features, literature, and monuments or knowledge about greetings and leave-takings, food preparation, and attitudes toward family life. The second type of goal is a heightened awareness of how to process information about another culture. Suggestions for the teaching of culture can be found in Chapter 4.

No matter how cultural knowledge is presented, it should be an integrated feature of the course, not an add-on. While "culture days" or other special events serve a function, they can tend to emphasize the exotic or become exaggerations of real life. On the other hand, careful inclusion of culture in reading selections can be a useful vehicle for imparting information and for furthering student skills in observing, problem solving, and hypothesizing.

In making decisions about what cultural elements to teach, teachers should be guided by the contexts, content areas, and functions that are already built into the curriculum. For example, food may be featured in the curriculum context for teaching particular grammar points, vocabulary, and so on. It should also serve as the context for teaching cultural information—for example, what types of food are served at each meal, at what times meals are eaten, the order in which foods are eaten, how guests are honored, and what gifts are appropriate for one's host. The purpose of this information should be to introduce students to a way of life that is varied, rich, and complete in itself.

Culture can also be linked with a number of linguistic functions. The functions of accepting, declining, thanking, and requesting are expressed in different ways according to the context. In the area of food, for example, students can learn culturally appropriate ways of accepting or declining second helpings, offering food, ordering a meal in a restaurant, and so on.

Students should know that having discrete pieces of information about another culture is not all they need to fit easily into another culture; they must also learn to observe the culture with as full a perspective as possible and avoid viewing cultures through "American glasses."

Reflections on the Role of Grammar

Until now we have said relatively little about the role of grammar, except to point out that traditional programs almost always place grammar at the center of the curriculum. Everything else—culture, vocabulary, listening comprehension, reading—is grafted onto it. In terms of learning, students who have achieved satisfactorily throughout the program will know a good deal about the foreign language grammar and probably more about the syntax of English as well. For the most part, however, they will not have assimilated the grammatical patterns in their speaking or writing.

We might well ask who has determined that the grammatical range of a language is either the possible or the proper content for a two- or three-year program of study. Historically, the grammatical focus of modern language study has its roots in the nineteenth century, when modern and classical languages were taught in much the same way. Objectives in those early modern language courses were related to the study of language for its own sake: analyzing and applying rules of grammar, learning vocabulary lists out of context, and translating with limited but achievable aims. Essentially, foreign language study was not seen as an end in itself. Instead, it was perceived as a mental disicipline, whose goal was to strengthen the general skills of analysis, memorization, and reasoning. These, in turn, were to be applied to the study of "important" subjects like philosophy and science. Once a smaller, more accessible world and a more linguistically and culturally diverse United States became a reality, the goals in the foreign language classroom shifted. Students, teachers, and the public expected language study to be practical and usable. These objectives, however, require different kinds of classroom concentration, and in embracing them, we added to the curricular demands without subtracting from the traditional grammatical syllabus. Those teachers who attempt to develop their students' proficiency find that the time available is insufficient. They have often coped by spreading the syllabus over another year. Others have succumbed to the outside pressure to "cover the book"—that is, all the grammar units—and have largely been forced to abandon the creative, the communicative, the involving, until later—by which time most students have already dropped the subject.

What are the curricular alternatives? In this chapter we have advocated a proficiency-based curriculum that places real-life communicative tasks at the center of the curriculum. Grammatical forms are selected for study at a time and to a degree of mastery that make sense in terms of the course objectives.

Another question that must be addressed is that of expectations of grammatical control. To have achieved the Green Book's basic outcomes in speaking, students must be comprehensible to native speakers used to dealing with foreigners. In listening and reading, they are expected to understand the gist of edited material or of short authentic texts that may be repeated or read several times. On the surface, only a minimal amount of grammatical control seems to be required. As experienced teachers know, however, a tremendous amount of time and effort are needed for students to learn, practice, and finally internalize structures to the point that they can be used spontaneously. This implies that the curriculum for each level must look forward to later levels of instruction, as well as consolidate the skills of the current level. Instruction at each level should not simply be oriented toward full control of the structures of that level but should aim for partial control, and in some cases only conceptual control, of structures that will be recycled through the curriculum for full control at higher levels.

All Four Skills or Selected Ones?

When foreign language teachers hear the terms *proficiency* and *proficiency-based curriculum*, their response is often to think only about oral proficiency. This is understandable, since proficiency testing has up to this point focused on oral skills. It is important to realize, however, that the concept of proficiency refers to all four skills. We can think about the skills of listening, reading, and writing as interwoven units of functions and contexts, just as we have come to do for speaking.

Except for occasional specialized courses, foreign language instruction in secondary schools concentrates on all four skills and culture. Generally, the term *four skills* has implied not only that speaking, listening, reading, and writing are all covered by the course but also that they receive equal emphasis in teaching and equal expectations in terms of outcomes. In reality, this is rarely the case, nor should it be. There are few classrooms where practice is meted out in equal doses; speaking, for instance, demands more concentrated and individual attention and develops more slowly than does reading, which can be practiced at home.

Teachers in the classroom may, for instructional purposes, choose to deal with the four skills separately, but in the real world of communication they are usually closely integrated. The curricular suggestions in *Academic Preparation in English* are built on this point. Every speaker requires a listener, readers often write about what they have read, and young people often read the lyrics as they listen to new songs. In an attempt to help students attain the Green Book outcomes, the teacher might decide that optimal levels in the various skills would more likely be met by observing an uneven but focused emphasis in the classroom. Sometimes this decision may have to do with expectations at colleges the students expect to attend. To take another example, if students from a particular high school tend to enter the job market directly after graduation, the curriculum should be designed to build stronger oral skills than written ones. This decision would be based on knowledge of the community and of the jobs students take. Ability in spoken Spanish for graduates seeking jobs in banking, medical work, retail establishments, and the like, in many areas of the United States would be a valuable, even necessary, ancillary skill. In other circumstances, students who have poor reading skills in English, but who resist remedial work, might be led to read more in another language. While there is no guarantee, there are reports from teachers who believe that underachieving students often come into the second-language class without the discouraging "baggage" they have acquired in subjects they have studied for a number of years.

Another rationale for variable skill emphasis is based on recent research in second-language acquisition that suggests that broader experience with receptive skills ("comprehensible input") may provide the necessary raw material for the eventual development of productive skills.[3] In practice, this means that a greater opportunity for hearing and reading language provides for a greater repertoire from which to draw speech and writing. Stephen Krashen calls this the Input Hypothesis; comprehensible input is language that is slightly above the level of the learner's control. Although research has not produced definitive results for curriculum planning, new importance has been given to listening comprehension by the Input Hypothesis and some experimental methods. The way has been opened for curriculum planners to consider placing greater emphasis on the receptive skills.

Another skill variable to consider in reorienting a four-skills curriculum might be reading. In recent times, as communicative approaches concentrated on developing oral skills, less time may have been allotted to reading. Speaking requires a high investment in instructional time to reach even the minimal outcomes stated in the Green Book. It is not uncommon to hear high school and college teachers alike bemoan lower standards and the inability of students to handle literature as they once did. What has been forgotten is that those students, who once entered literature courses at earlier stages and seemingly performed in a superior fashion, had little in the way of oral proficiency.

In short sequences a choice has to be made so that some usable level of language is reached in at least one skill area. An additional limitation on speaking may involve class sizes that do not allow the necessary time and individualized attention needed to develop speaking skills. There may be languages and groups of students who would benefit from a curriculum that maximizes their reading proficiency and leaves the opportunity for oral expression until another time.

In summary, even though texts and basic materials stress a four-

---

3. Stephen D. Krashen, *Second Language Acquisition and Second Language Learning* (Oxford and New York: Pergamon Press, 1981).

skills approach, the curriculum can be designed and managed so that selected skills are emphasized. The rationale for reaching that decision should be based on student needs and interests and should recognize the constraints and goals of the local district. It should take into account the expectations of the colleges the students will be attending. Emphasizing selected skills should not diminish achievement of the Green Book outcomes; it should help some students surpass that level in one or more of the skills.

Curriculum for the Lower Grades

Certainly, while the preponderance of foreign language programs in this country is located in high schools, a fair number do serve junior high school students in grades 7 and 8 as well. These junior high or middle school courses are often spread over a two-year period, so that seventh graders meet for three days a week and eighth graders for four days a week. This allows the teacher to adapt the material more appropriately to the younger learner, to emphasize oral skills, and to encourage participation in interesting cultural activities.

The curricular content of courses for seventh graders should be different from that of a first-year language course offered to ninth- or tenth-grade students. Students who start language study at age 12 or 13 need courses in which the balance among the four skills, the depth of content, the culture topics, and the classroom activities are appropriate for their interests and attention span. Unfortunately, when such students move from junior to senior high school, especially if this involves a physical movement from one building to another, they are often placed in classes with students who have begun language study at age 15. They end up almost starting language study over again. Cooperation between junior high or middle schools and high schools can make sure that students keep moving forward, rather than revisiting material they have already learned.

One of the peculiar features of language study at the junior high school level is that it is usually offered to students who have already proved themselves to be academically strong, particularly in the area of verbal skills and language arts. Schools should realize that the opposite policy can significantly contribute to building educational equality. There is a growing body of evidence that foreign language study would benefit students with a weak background in language arts. Insights into how language systems operate and an expanded vocabulary constitute two valuable outcomes. In addition, the opportunity to enjoy a more slowly paced first course, and to have a longer sequence, should enhance the chance for success of the more average student. This argument was advanced by a member of the Baltimore City School Board, Robert L. Walker, in his support of a foreign language requirement for all students, not just the college-bound.[4]

Other Models

This section describes two kinds of language programs that differ from traditional courses. One of their attractions is that they create interest in foreign language study because students who participate are more likely to begin language study earlier and to continue for a longer period of time. Although these programs typically occur in elementary and middle schools, high school teachers can profit from an understanding of their strengths and limitations. These considerations will be important in designing high school foreign language programs.

Exploratory Programs

Exploratory programs essentially comprise courses in which different languages and language systems are surveyed. They introduce students in elementary or middle schools to foreign language by offering them a first experience with one or more languages. Various models exist, but there is a consensus about overall goals. As set forth by Alice Omaggio et al., these goals include the following:[5]

---

4. "Foreign Languages in Baltimore and Cincinnati," *Modern Language Journal* 68 (1984): 27.

5. Alice C. Omaggio et al., "Foreign Language in the Secondary School: Reconciling the Dream with the Reality," in *Foreign Languages: Key Links in the Chain of Learning,* ed. Robert G. Mead, Jr. (Middlebury, Vermont: Northeast Conference, 1983), pp. 26–53.

1. To establish a basis for eventual proficiency in a foreign language
2. To generate interest in and receptivity to the study of another language
3. To sensitize students to the rationale for foreign language study
4. To dispel fears and misconceptions about foreign language
5. To make language study available to more students
6. To aid students in making the decision about which language to study

The ideal placement of exploratory courses is one year before the earliest year for which a commitment to full-time language study can be made. Students who may have been afraid to attempt a full-scale language course could instead be attracted to, and gain confidence and interest in, a lower-pressure exploratory program. It is important that the experiences with various languages be parallel, however, so that decisions about which language to study can be based on factors other than the "nicest" or the "easiest" teacher, the course that involves an outing to a restaurant, and so on. In many schools these programs are successful because teachers have worked together to produce a curriculum that is equivalent in scope, while maintaining the flavor and special features of the various languages.

Immersion Programs

Immersion programs refer to those elementary school programs that use a foreign language to teach content in other subjects. Total immersion programs, modeled largely on those developed in Canada, begin by having kindergarten-age youngsters play, learn their numbers and colors, and listen to the teacher, all in the foreign language. Formal language instruction begins later, usually in the third grade. Partial immersion programs are characterized by a split day in which the native language is the medium of instruction for approximately half the time, and the foreign language for the rest. The research data are now extensive enough to confirm that there are no negative results in achievement as far as the other academic subjects are concerned. Indeed, the evidence suggests that achievement in course content by students in immersion programs equals or surpasses that of their peers who receive instruction in only their native language. A significant characteristic of these data is that they encompass urban and integrated populations as well. Immersion has been a successful vehicle of several of the magnet school programs in large cities.

The immersion program requires no special curriculum, for it simply delivers the regular curriculum of the elementary program in a foreign language. This is a far cry from the traditional Foreign Language in the Elementary School (FLES) programs that devoted a few class sessions a week to foreign language learning. While the FLES programs also exist in some of today's schools, interdisciplinary and immersion models have replaced them as innovations that are revitalizing foreign language in the elementary schools. High schools will soon have the challenge of meeting the needs of some students who enter with many years of language study. If these programs become widespread, even stronger proficiency standards may appear someday as part of the discussion of academic preparation for college. What is being accomplished today with foreign language study is only a fraction of what can be done tomorrow.

Latin in the Early Grades

A renaissance of sorts has taken place in the study of Latin in recent years, and much of the activity has centered on the elementary school curriculum. Grades 4 through 6 have proved to be an excellent time to begin the study of a classical language. These formative years are ideal for building a foundation for future modern language study as well as a solid basis for improved native language skills. The largest elementary school Latin programs have been situated in large urban systems: Philadelphia, New York, Washington, D.C., Los Angeles. They have been responsible for introducing foreign language to students who might otherwise have missed the chance, and in addition they have provided these students with valuable general academic skills.

The greatest impediment to a strong Latin curriculum in many schools has been a shortage of teachers. As the appeal of Latin, especially as the first foreign language, increases, the pool of teachers decreases with few replacements in sight. A successful project geared to address this problem is in operation in Philadelphia.[6] This staff development project prepared both elementary classroom teachers and secondary teachers of English in the use of specific Latin materials for their students. These teachers took courses at cooperating universities and participated in follow-up workshops. The outcomes for their students were impressive: a control group–experimental group comparison demonstrated that the students with Latin outperformed the others on the Reading Comprehension subtest of the California Achievement Test. In a very real way, these new Latin courses serve as a head start; while they benefit all students, their greatest impact is ultimately felt by students who may have had difficulty acquiring an equal footing with other youngsters. These students enjoy a foreign language experience that opens doors to a greater mastery of their own and of a new language.

Conclusion

This chapter has dealt with curriculum as a process, not as a simple document. Some of the questions that we invite foreign language teachers to ask as they design their curricula are those that teachers of other subjects might well ask as they design programs: What kind of program does the community want? How does this subject area contribute to the overall educational goals of the community? What skill areas should receive the greatest emphasis? What should students be able to do by the end of a particular course?

We have included a section on the role of grammar because our view of how grammar fits into a language program differs significantly from the traditional one. Students will not speak or read or write less accurately when they are instructed in a proficiency-based curriculum. On the contrary, they will be able to put their knowledge of grammar to immediate use because the structures taught will be relevant for the functional tasks that are at the center of the curriculum.

---

6. Rudolph Masciantonio, "Language Arts through Latin: A Staff Development Project," *Foreign Language Annals* 16 (1983): 369–372.

We have also sketched out curricula for the lower grades, where foreign language often is not taught at all. We hope to stimulate discussion about the adaptability of language programs for younger children as well as to underscore the value of high school teachers taking the possibilities of such programs into account.

The motif that reappears throughout the chapter is, once again, that of proficiency. When functional language tasks are set as the goal of a program of study, the curriculum must provide a plan whereby students can attain these outcomes. The classroom strategies discussed in Chapter 4, therefore, are oriented toward making the student an independent, proficient user of another language.

IV. Teaching Foreign Language

The purpose of this chapter is to present some applications of the ideas outlined in Chapters 2 and 3. In Chapter 2 we discussed desired outcomes for high school language programs, and in Chapter 3 we described a process that leads from the outcomes to curricula for particular courses. This chapter goes one step closer to the students and presents suggestions and strategies for achieving specific teaching goals.

We do not intend these applications to be prescriptive, for we know that pronouncements on how a language, or a particular aspect of a language, should be taught are seldom useful. Teachers develop new ideas and strategies through their own experience with students, through their discussion with colleagues, and through their reading. We hope that the examples presented in this chapter will serve as food for thought in that process of development. Once teachers in a school or a district have agreed on the goals of instruction and have a curriculum in place that is designed to reach those goals, the next step is to decide on the techniques and activities in the classroom that will lead students to the desired goals.

The foreign language field has experienced the extremes in methodology during the last 60 years. We have embraced prescriptive methods, such as audiolingualism or the direct method, which spelled out procedures in a step-by-step manner. We have also observed a number of idiosyncratic approaches that owed their effectiveness to a single teacher's (or a group of teachers') special skills. Between these positions, many approaches have evolved that have their foundation in a specific psychological orientation. These include the broad methods, such as cognitive, communicative, humanistic, and individualized instruction, as well as the methods usually associated with an individual, such as Asher's Total Physical Response, Curran's Counseling (or Community) Language

Learning, Gattegno's Silent Way, and Lozanov's Suggestopedia.[1]

We have learned from the many methods that have been tried in recent decades that there is no single way to teach a foreign language that will suit all students and teachers. Not all learners are alike, and individual abilities, learning styles, ages, and attitudes will require different instructional strategies. Likewise, teachers' personalities and experience will mesh better with some methods than with others. Finally, as research teaches us more about the language learning process, methodology will continue to evolve as we try to implement those findings in classroom activities.

There are both advantages and disadvantages in being able to choose among many methods. In one sense, it is easier to be handed a prescription, complete with all the directions for use. On the other hand, the opportunity to find ideas that work and to carry them into practice gives teachers great freedom. It seems reasonable and fruitful to approach pedagogical issues with an open but critical mind, to experiment with a keen eye on objectives, and to choose those practices which best suit teacher, student, level, curriculum, school, and environment. In fact, recent research concerning proficiency levels suggests that teachers may need to change their approach for each new stage of learning. Rather than pursuing a search for the one best method, we might begin to look for the best matches between a method and a given level of student achievement. The suggestions in this chapter have been selected for their theoretical and practical relevance to the specific *Academic Preparation for College* outcomes in foreign language and to the Basic Academic Competencies. We hope that the suggestions and examples given here will serve as a starting point for discussions among teachers to develop additional strategies and activities.

Teaching the Language Components

Language teaching involves focusing on two areas: (1) the elements of language, that is, vocabulary, structure, sounds, and so forth;

---

1. For a brief descriptive overview of all these methods, see David P. Benseler and Renate A. Schulz, "Methodological Trends in College Foreign Language Instruction," *Modern Language Journal* 64 (1980): 88–96.

(2) the four skills, which use these elements to produce or receive meaningful language. The Green Book outcomes are stated in terms of skills and culture and do not directly mention grammar and vocabulary. Yet our texts and the everyday business of foreign language teaching revolve around these building blocks of the language system itself. Our discussion of teaching strategies begins with suggestions for teaching vocabulary and grammar to show how students might acquire the resources necessary for carrying out the language tasks outlined in the Green Book outcome statements.

Vocabulary: The Key to Meaning

Which communicates more?

1. "The kignet was dieben to the svockler."
2. "dog boy bark"

The first sentence has a meaningful structure; we know the agent, the recipient of the action, and that the act was completed. But since the content words are nonsensical, the sentence carries no message. In the second case the bare minimum exists; words are listed in dictionary form with no syntactic connections. But we can certainly guess at the meaning of the three words and provide a logical interpretation. It is vocabulary, not grammatical correctness, that enables us to fill in the gaps of an incomplete idea. The mind uses natural relationships to associate the words. At the beginning levels, when simple, basic communication is the goal, vocabulary carries the weight of meaning. While this *moi vouloir pain* language is not appropriate as a long-range objective, it has great communicative value at beginning levels of instruction. Beginning students who learn a number of grammatical patterns with minimal vocabulary will not be able to communicate, even inaccurately. This imbalance between vocabulary and grammar lay behind one of the drawbacks of audiolingualism. The emphasis in early levels of audiolingual instruction focused on drill and mastery of structures while vocabulary played a secondary role. When students later attempted to construct their own thoughts in the foreign language, they were often stopped by an inadequate vocabulary.

Several basic principles should be kept in mind when teaching the vocabulary necessary to perform the language tasks contained in the Green Book outcomes.

1. Students need to acquire an active personalized vocabulary, since the outcomes for speaking state that students should be able to deal with familiar topics and areas of immediate need.
2. Students' writing vocabulary also should be adequate to cover the same topics.
3. Vocabulary should be learned and practiced in practical and relevant theme groups.
4. Students should learn receptive, or recognition, vocabulary for listening and reading that is broader than the vocabulary they can control in speaking and writing.

The next section deals with three phases of vocabulary development: presentation, practice, and expansion.

The Case for Personalized Vocabulary

Space limitations and other practical considerations oblige textbook authors and publishers to present relatively short vocabulary lists in each chapter. Many current texts have organized the vocabulary in thematic groups, such as family, sports, food, clothing, school. Some of these presentations are largely visual and attractive so that students can grasp the meanings of new words without direct reference to an English-language equivalent. The selection of words in a particular textbook, however, may be too general to be useful or may not include words that students need to talk or write about their own lives. No matter how good the textbook may be, teachers will still have to supplement it with words and expressions that emerge from students' own perceived vocabulary needs.

For example, in most, if not all, textbooks the vocabulary in the unit on family relationships seems to assume that students come from nuclear families with siblings close to one another in age. Young people from family groups that include stepparents, half brothers or half sisters, brothers-in-law or sisters-in-law, nieces or nephews, will find themselves lacking needed vocabulary in class activities on this topic. Similarly, the units on sports or foods can never hope to provide sufficient vocabulary so that all students can list their preferences. The words they need must be supplied by the teacher.

Vocabulary needs may go beyond the individual student to the area where the students live. Teachers of students in western Texas or in New York City will need to emphasize different vocabulary even when teaching expressions for climate and weather. Students in the Pacific Northwest can use vocabulary for drizzle, downpour, fog, and mist, which would be less relevant for students in Arizona.

By the time students reach the level of the advanced outcomes, they have active vocabularies that go beyond their immediate personal experiences. As they progress toward the basic outcomes, however, students need to move beyond the vocabulary that the textbook presents for the average audience to words that will serve their own communicative purposes.

Presenting Personalized Vocabulary

Using the vocabulary presented by the textbook as a common core that all students are expected to know, the teacher can help students develop their own personal vocabulary for each thematic unit or activity. For example, if a class is working on family trees as a way to practice writing the names of family members, the teacher can ask the class what words they will need. As the words are called out, the teacher writes them and the foreign language equivalent on the board. Each student takes from the list what he or she needs.

The area of occupations and professions is one in which a personalized vocabulary is surely needed. Textbooks cover such jobs as teacher, doctor, and secretary, but most students need a different vocabulary to say how their adult relatives make a living. The topic generally arises when students are asking and answering questions about their families. Before the activities begin, the teacher can follow the same procedure of writing on the board the names of occupations that students need. The students can be held responsible for learning this vocabulary if they are asked on tests to write or talk about these topics in the same personal way they have done in class.

Students can be asked to keep a notebook in which they write words they want to learn. The teacher can make homework assignments based on these words—for example, having students look up their meanings, make vocabulary cards, and use the words in sentences or paragraphs.

Practicing Vocabulary

While textbooks contain many exercises, most practice concentrates on grammar topics. Only a few textbooks have systematically included practice exercises to assist learners in remembering the meanings of words. Indeed, when students are asked how they study vocabulary words, they generally say, "I memorize them." Words learned out of context are quickly forgotten; effective learning requires meaningful practice. If students have sufficient work with vocabulary in context, they will be able to learn words without resorting to rote memorization.

Increased classroom vocabulary practice is especially necessary for students who are not expert at rote memorization. Most, if not all, of these students *can* learn a language; they may need more time and instructional help to do so. While creative teaching and meaningful practice serve all students well, these students are most in need of contexts in which the practice of particular lexical items makes sense.

Exercises in which there is a real information gap can give students practice in using personalized vocabulary. This makes it immediately obvious what additional vocabulary students need to talk about themselves. Much classroom vocabulary practice involves having the students respond to questions whose answers are already known by everyone—for example, "What color is Susan's dress?" "What time is it?" This is pseudocommunication at best, with no attempt to combine language practice with any meaningful exchange of information or feelings. Students could be practicing vocabulary with questions like "What is your favorite color?" "What clothes do you have in that color?" "What time does your family eat dinner?" "What time did you get home yesterday?" The exchange of real information can be motivating to both questioner and respondent in a way that "What color is your shirt?" can never be.

The information-gap principle can provide the starting point for vocabulary exercises in which part of a group has information that the other part needs. The familiar Twenty Questions, in which students figure out the identity of the teacher or one of their classmates by asking yes-no questions (Are you an American? Are you a woman? Are you alive? Are you a basketball player?), can be expanded to objects (Is it round? Is it heavy? Is it black?) or to places (Is it a city? Is it in Africa? Is it in the South?). Another exercise involves having students complete a map or place people and objects in a room by asking questions of and receiving directions from the students who have the information.

Expanding Vocabulary

Students who learn words one by one find vocabulary building a slow and often painful process. Two techniques will help expand their vocabularies more quickly: (1) vocabulary-expansion exercises that concentrate on a particular content area, so that students very quickly learn many words about one subject; (2) exercises that give information about, and practice in applying, word patterns and cognitive strategies to figure out the meanings of new words.

Almost any area can serve as the basis for vocabulary-expansion exercises. The exercises should be simple in format, so that students do not have to concentrate on the grammatical form of the response. Here is an example of an oral vocabulary-expansion exercise that teaches students the names of foods.

The teacher asks the students to think of their favorite food. They should have a second choice in reserve, because no repetition of food items from one student to another is allowed. Food items must be specific, not generic. "Meat" is not acceptable, but "ham" or "chicken" is. This requirement will give the teacher occasions to ask if students need help with words. The demonstration goes as follows:

Teacher: Susan, what do you like?

Susan: I like pizza. John, what do you like?

John: I like chocolate ice cream.

Teacher: David, who likes pizza?

David: Susan likes pizza.

As more students are drawn in, interest mounts because the favorite foods of earlier respondents are recycled into the exercise. Students interpret the exercise as a memory game, but as they work to remember what their classmates said previously, they are also learning and practicing the names of twenty to twenty-five food items. The form of the exercise is constant, involving only two sentence patterns, so students can give most of their attention to hearing, remembering, and producing the information provided by other students.

Authentic texts are also valuable for vocabulary-expansion exercises. A menu is an obvious document to use to expand students' repertoire of food items. Class schedules of students in other countries provide a basis to learn the names of school subjects. Students can use blank schedules to fill in their own courses or those of their siblings or friends.

A second approach to expanding students' vocabulary, particularly in reading, involves cognitive strategies for vocabulary recognition. Students can learn to be on the alert for cognates and word families. They can learn to analyze the context to figure out the meanings of new words. If students have these skills in their native language, the skills may at best be dormant. Foreign language teachers can make them into conscious processes that will serve the students both in the foreign language and in English. The textbook probably will treat this area lightly, if at all, and the teacher will have to create or adapt supplementary materials.

Let us take as an example a word like *jaunir* (to turn yellow) in French, which almost certainly will be unfamiliar to students. The word *jaunir* can be used as the pivot for providing in context a set of related sentences. They could employ the words *rougir* (to turn red or to blush), *noircir* (to turn black), *brunir* (to turn brown), *blanchir* (to turn white). Students should be led to generalize that colors in French become verbs with the addition of *-ir*. Numerous examples in all languages can be drawn from almost any spoken or printed passage. The long-range goal is that students encountering new words such as *bleuir* will be able to make more sensible and correct guesses.

Grammar: An Old Means to a New End

In Chapter 3 we discussed the role of grammar in the curriculum and held that communicative linguistic functions, not the grammar of a language, must be placed at the center of a proficiency-based curriculum. Grammar is one of many tools in effective communication, not the only one. Learners should control structures in order to use them to convey their message and to understand what they hear and read. Mastery of grammar in terms of being able to recite rules and manipulate patterns out of context should not be mistaken for mastery or for attainment of a particular level of proficiency. Knowledge of grammar for its own sake should not be a long-range instructional objective. Performance, not knowledge alone, counts, and while knowledge certainly contributes to performance, it is not sufficient by itself. Because grammar is still at the core of most textbooks, teachers will face the challenge of making major changes in how the grammar is presented and practiced.

To assure that grammar assumes a proper supporting role in the curriculum, several questions must be addressed:

1. How can we link grammar to the larger language tasks and purposes inherent in communication?
2. What is a reasonable sequence for grammar coverage at various levels of instruction?
3. What kind of exercises promote the transfer of skills from classroom practice to real-world use?

Linking Grammar and Communication: Deciding What Grammar to Teach

In this section we return to a point made in Chapter 3: the most effective way to teach grammar is through a *spiraling* approach. This involves several introductions and treatments of a given structure, first for concept control, second for receptive control, and finally for partial and then full productive control. The rationale behind this approach is that students need time to assimilate new language patterns. If they are presented with too much grammar too quickly, they may end up knowing a good deal about the language, but they will be able to use very little of it. A spiraling approach gives students intensive practice with a smaller amount of grammatical material while they are introduced to new material on a conceptual or receptive plane. They have more time to assimilate what they are learning and to develop greater overall language skill.

Most major textbooks take a linear approach to grammar, not a spiraling one. Each grammatical topic receives extensive and intensive treatment over a short period of time. The uses of the dative in Russian are covered in two weeks; or all of the forms, meanings, and uses of *ser* and *estar* in Spanish are presented in one or two chapters. The result is that as students focus on one and then another grammar point, they lose what they have already covered. Hundreds of oral proficiency interviews with high school and college students have demonstrated that relatively few of the grammar points studied in the classroom have been integrated into the students' speaking skills. This implies that we need to rethink our expectations for student performance and to reevaluate our purpose in teaching the more advanced structures.

The spiraling approach consists of coverage purposefully meted out in manageable doses and tied to specific meanings. Review takes on a positive face as the learner returns to a topic to add to a knowledge base rather than to retrieve what was incompletely mastered.[2]

A major assumption of this technique is that the various meanings included in a single grammar point are not equally useful for communication goals. For the classroom, teachers decide about the most critical meanings based on students' level and communication needs. As an elementary example, students in Spanish and French classes may need to learn very soon how to introduce themselves: "Me llamo Felicia" or "Je m'appelle Philippe." That students are taught to use a reflexive form for a particular purpose does not mean they have to learn about the whole reflexive system. This same approach, teaching parts of structures for a given purpose and saving other parts for a later time, can be applied to many elements of the grammatical core. In addition, teachers will probably want to teach some items for productive, and others for receptive, mastery, especially where alternative structures communicate the same meaning.

Teachers who use this method will have to make decisions about how to reorder and refocus the presentation of grammar. Galloway has suggested the following principles for making these decisions:[3]

1. Can parts of the element be introduced first as lexical items and later expanded and treated structurally?
2. Is this element used more in reading and listening than in production? Can it be presented first for recognition and later for production?
3. Can aspects of the concept be broken down and presented in a spiral fashion?

---

2. The handbook *Functional-Notional Concepts: Adapting the FL Textbook*, by Gail Guntermann and June K. Phillips (Language in Education Series, no. 44, Washington, D.C.: Center for Applied Linguistics, 1982), has suggestions for adapting the grammatical points in textbooks and many examples of purposeful language activities.

3. Vicki B. Galloway in Frank W. Medley, Jr., "Designing the Proficiency-Based Curriculum," pp. 13–39.

4. Can the element be presented first for manipulation and later (in a subsequent unit) for communicative use?
5. Can the element be presented first as a concept and reintroduced later for partial, and then finally full, control?
6. Has there been sufficient "distancing" of complex concepts to allow students a processing period?
7. Can this item be postponed because it duplicates the function of another item?

The students themselves and their desire to communicate in another language are an important resource for teachers. With the traditional grammatical syllabus, students were seldom directed to think about the possible functional uses of the structures they were learning. Lessons can become more purposeful and interesting to students if they know what they might do with them later.

Let us take an example of how a grammar topic might be integrated into the language function that it supports so that its purpose is more obvious to the student:

Function: Description

Content: Physical characteristics of people

Grammar point: Descriptive adjectives

Skills: Reading and writing

Description of activity: Students are given photographs of missing persons. They are asked to write all points bulletins (APBs) describing these persons, using as many adjectives as they know. Photos are then mounted on the bulletin board, and the APBs are shuffled and passed out to members of the class. (This can be done a day or two later if the teacher wishes to correct students' drafts.) The class then tries to match the bulletins with the photographs. The activity can be expanded to four skills by having one student play the role of a family member who reports a missing person to another student playing the role of a police officer; the second student then transforms the oral description into a written one.[4]

This framework can be used with any grammar point that is purposeful for students, given their stage of proficiency in the foreign

---

4. Guntermann and Phillips, *Functional-Notional Concepts,* p. 48.

language. If aspects of a particular grammatical topic in the text do not lend themselves to a communicative task, that is a signal to the teacher that it should be passed by or receive less emphasis at this point in the course. By no means do any of these suggestions imply that grammar is not important. The real importance of grammar lies in its potential for communication. When teachers adapt the grammar in this fashion, students who do not have high-level skills in their native language will not be at a disadvantage. They can learn the usages of a foreign language even though they may be less skilled in analyzing formal patterns.

Practicing Grammatical Patterns

In the previous section we discussed the spiraling approach to the presentation of grammar, in which grammar points are broken down into their component parts and introduced over a longer period of time for successively greater degrees of control. Once the material has been introduced, how can it be practiced so as to lead to proficiency—the ability to use the material creatively in context, not just in the drills in which the material was originally presented? A progression of drill stages, such as that proposed by Paulston and Selekman, can be helpful in weaning students from reliance on drill patterns and giving them practice in more independent communication. This model identifies three stages of drill practice:[5]

- *Manipulative (mechanical) drills* have one correct response. Learners respond and practice whether or not they understand the meaning of what they are saying. Their response demonstrates that they are learning habits and automatic responses. The focus is on form, the correct manipulation of the pattern. Example: "Do you play sports?" Response: "Yes, I play sports."

- *Meaningful drills* allow the teacher to retain control of the form being practiced, but the student provides the content of the answer. Although the students must understand the question before they can respond, the focus is still on manipulation of structures. Example: "What sports do you play?" Response: "I play (basketball, baseball, hockey)."

---

5. Christina Bratt Paulston and Howard R. Selekman, "Interaction Activities in the Foreign Language Classroom," *Foreign Language Annals* 9 (1976): 249–250.

- *Communicative drills* still revolve around a discrete structure, but the response approaches real communication in that the focus is on meaning. Although the form of the answer can be predicted by the topic of the drill, only the student can supply the information in the answer. Example: "Tell me about your favorite sport." Response: "I play a lot of basketball. I prefer defense because . . ."

Examples of these three kinds of drills for a grammar lesson on the imperative might include the following.

Manipulative: Change the following sentences to the command form as you give a friend directions.

Sentence	Response
1. You cross the street.	Cross the street.
2. You walk two blocks.	Walk two blocks.
3. You turn left at the light.	Turn left at the light.
4. You look for a yellow house.	Look for a yellow house.

Note that the student can do well whether the sentence is understood or not. What is being asked in each case is that students manipulate the elements of the sentence. The transformation is the same each time.

Meaningful: The members of the Stevens family all have problems. In each of the following sentences, give the person the most appropriate command.

Sentence	Response
1. John's clothes are dirty.	John, wash your clothes; *or* John, change your clothes.
2. Susan is tired.	Susan, go to bed; *or* Susan, lie down for a while.
3. Eleanor is hungry. Dinner is on the table.	Eleanor, eat your dinner; *or* Eleanor, come to the table.
4. Sam wants to go to the school dance, but he has a lot of homework.	Sam, do your homework now; *or* Sam, go to the dance later.

Notice that the instructor controls the form of the response (a short command is the most appropriate response), but that the students provide the content of the command. Students must understand the stimulus sentences in order to respond. It is not enough just to manipulate the structure.

Communicative: You write an advice column for the local newspaper. For each problem sent to you, give your best advice. Use your imagination.

Sentence	*Response*
1. I like a boy in my math class. What should I do to get his attention?	Invite him to eat lunch with you; send him a card; other.
2. My parents are very strict. How can I get more freedom?	Be cooperative and helpful; talk to your parents about the problem; other.
3. I failed two subjects this term. How can I improve my grades?	Study every night; organize your notebooks; take good notes; other.
4. My little sister wants to go everywhere with me. What can I do?	Talk to your parents; spend some time with your sister each week; other.

In the communicative drill the students control the form and the content of the responses. The form of the stimulus invites students to continue to practice command forms, but the communicative nature of the exercise allows them to use appropriate linguistic forms other than commands if they so desire. The focus of the drill is on meaning, as students see how the grammar they are learning is used.

Textbooks have changed a great deal since the days of audiolingualism, when they were oriented around standard sets of grammatical exercises. They now contain fewer purely manipulative drills and far more communicative activities. Teachers should carefully evaluate the exercises in their textbooks to see whether they follow the progression outlined above. The sequence with each structure and perhaps even in each class period, from manipulative to meaningful to communicative, should be one that supports students as they move toward free and confident expression in the foreign language.

As teachers examine their texts with these three types of drills in mind, they may well find that most of the exercises are of the manipulative type. The teacher will then have to supplement the text with more meaningful and communicative drills if proficiency outcomes, such as those stated in the Green Book, are the instructional goal.

The purpose of manipulative drills is to focus on repetition of linguistic forms. They can certainly be made more interesting for students if the teacher creates a context into which the practice of grammatical forms can fit. The same kind of intensive practice with grammatical forms can also be accomplished via meaningful drills if they are carefully set up and controlled. One advantage of meaningful drills is that they are more interesting to students, because they allow for more personalized responses and for a real exchange of information.

A Note on Error Correction

No discussion of grammar drills and communicative activities would be complete without some recommendations on error correction. Most teachers correct errors systematically and probably almost automatically when students speak. This comes from a desire to have students hear only correct speech patterns. On the other hand, it is important to encourage students to function independently, without relying on the teacher to correct errors and supply words.

As classroom exercises move from manipulative to communicative, the teacher's role should become less obvious. The teacher should correct students when they are concentrating on linguistic forms in structured drills, because it is important that students form and practice habits of correct pronunciation, intonation, and grammar. When students are engaged in communicative activities that focus on meaning, however, the teacher's role should be to observe the errors rather than to correct them on the spot. The correction should come later, perhaps in the form of a manipulative or a meaningful drill of points that most students had trouble with in the communicative exercises. The importance of delaying the correction is that students are encouraged to treat the oral interaction as real communication, and not as a pretext for a grammar lesson. The exchange of information in the student-to-student interaction provides greater motivation for communication than any pattern drill ever can.

Spiraling and the Latin Curriculum

The notion of a spiral approach to grammar is just as appropriate to Latin as to other languages. Latin students, too, need time to assimilate the information required to describe and control this language that is so different from English. In fact, a spiral approach would do much to alleviate the most frequently raised criticisms of the teaching of Latin grammar—namely, that it can be an endless stream of details that have few unifying themes or concepts, and that important elements could be better learned if they could be acquired over a longer period of time. Whether the time is long or short, we can be more effective when we sequence concept control, receptive control, and productive control.

At the level of concept control, students need to know how the new structure fits into the overall context of learning—that is, how it relates to what has already been learned and, sometimes, what will be learned. This demands that instructors provide a practical and theoretically sound description of Latin within a few broad categories, each of which has subcategories, and so on. Thus, for example, an introduction to the ablative absolute might place it first within the broad category of modifiers, then adverbial modifiers (in contrast to adjectival modifiers). In this way, students learn how the new structure relates to the sentence as a whole. The teacher might show how the ablative absolute adds the same kind of information as other adverbial modifiers, such as adverbs, prepositional phrases, and some subordinate clauses. Other teachers may select a concept that relates the ablative absolute to participle uses or dependent clause types (this one being a nonfinite dependent clause), or to the uses of the ablative case. Some categorizations, of course, provide greater opportunities for specific elaboration than others.

Receptive control can be achieved as the learners proceed to a series of explanations and exercises that insure that they can recognize the structure and its critical features and can discriminate it from non-ablative absolute structures. Productive control is achieved later, when learners have all the skills necessary to understand its full meaning when meeting it in reading, translating it accurately from Latin to English, or, possibly, recognizing English clauses expressed by the ablative absolute in Latin.

Teaching the Four Skills and Culture

We have just discussed vocabulary and grammar as two distinct components of foreign language teaching, but this separation is for instructional emphasis only. The outcomes listed in the Green Book clearly refer to language skills in terms of communication by indicating what students should be able (1) to understand by listening and reading, (2) to express through speaking and writing, and (3) how they should be able to interact with members of the particular language culture. It is sometimes useful for purposes of discussion to combine skills according to oral and written forms. For teaching and learning purposes, however, thinking in terms of receptive and productive skills parallels the mental processes the learner must control. It is also important to integrate the teaching of language skills with instruction about the cultures of native speakers of the language.

The progression of drills from manipulative to communicative is similar to the distinction made by Wilga Rivers between skill-getting and skill-using activities.[6,7] Skill-getting activities are designed to give students the skills they need to communicate. They include explanations of grammar points, instruction and practice in guessing meaning from context, instruction about factual aspects of the culture, manipulative and meaningful drills of the type described above, and simulated conversation. (Rivers calls this pseudo-

---

6. Wilga M. Rivers, *A Practical Guide to the Teaching of French* (New York: Oxford University Press, 1975).

7. Wilga M. Rivers, "A New Curriculum for New Purposes," *Foreign Language Annals* 18 (1985): 37–47.

communication.[8]) Skill-using activities, which include such things as communicative drills, small-group activities, culture-oriented role plays, and skimming and scanning of printed selections, are designed to let students use what they have learned to communicate with each other and to get information from printed or oral texts.

As teachers work with their students on the development of the four skills, they will move smoothly from skill-getting to skill-using activities. As stated above, the progression will be much like the one from manipulative to communicative drills described earlier.

Strategies for Teaching Culture

Strategies for teaching culture can be divided into two main categories: (1) ways to provide students with information about other cultures, and (2) ways to develop students' ability to "process" other cultures without reference to their own.

The *lecture* is a time-honored way to transmit information to students. The most frequent cause for the failure of lectures as a teaching strategy is that they are a passive experience for students. It is easy for students to lose concentration if they are not directed in their listening. Accompanying visuals can help focus students' attention, as can a previously discussed list of questions that the lecture will help them answer. Relatively brief lectures in which students must take notes and which are followed by discussion or other follow-up activities will be the most successful.

Observational dialogues involve having students watch a videotape or live dialogue (best performed by two teachers or advanced students) to learn about an aspect of the target culture. After observing the dialogue, students might be asked to carry out one or more activities: summarize what took place, describe the relationship between the speakers, and identify the linguistic or other cues that helped make the relationship clear. There are a variety of possibilities.

---

8. Wilga M. Rivers, *Communicating Naturally in a Second Language: Theory and Practice in Language Teaching* (Cambridge, England: Cambridge University Press, 1983).

Audiomotor units combine linguistic and cultural features. A unit consists of a number of commands that revolve around a particular theme, such as table manners, greetings, or introductions. The teacher reads the commands, models the culturally appropriate behavior, and then asks students to pantomime the behaviors. These units have the advantage of integrating the acquisition of cultural information with vocabulary building, listening comprehension practice, and learning and practicing appropriate gestures.

Helping students develop skills for understanding what they observe in another culture is more complex than conveying information about the culture. The phenomenon of "culture shock" arises largely from the seemingly constant confrontation between one's expectations and actual events and personal interactions in the target culture. If students can learn not to expect daily events to mean what they mean in the home culture, they will have a much easier adjustment to traveling or living abroad, or to working or living in ethnic communities in the United States.

Culture assimilators are scenarios that depict interaction between a member of the target culture and a nonnative (usually an American). The situation presents a miscommunication or confusion on the part of the American, and the students' task is to figure out what went wrong and why. Programmed culture assimilators are followed by four plausible explanations of the behavior described in the episode. Students who approach the scenario with an American perspective select the wrong explanation. After getting feedback from the teacher or through class discussion, they try again. Students eventually realize that expectations that members of other cultures operate with the same assumptions Americans have can lead to misinterpretation of the scenario. This consciousness raising is the first step toward learning how to experience another culture without the distortion of one's own cultural assumptions.

Cultural assimilators are a valuable classroom activity for several reasons. They are both easy to write and can take little time to present to students. If the teacher chooses not to have the class engage in discussion about the possible explanations, one can be worked through in five minutes or less. They are powerful tools for developing the Basic Academic Competencies of reasoning and observing.

Mini-dramas are like extended cultural assimilators, and are used in the same way. They enable students to recognize, confront, and analyze their cultural assumptions. They consist of several scenes that describe cross-cultural misunderstandings that result in miscommunication, confusion, or even hostility. At various points during the mini-drama, the teacher stops the action and engages the students in discussion about what is causing the misunderstanding. Seelye[9] has several examples of mini-dramas that involve purchasing fruit from a street vendor in France, the etiquette of restaurant dining in Germany, and child–adult interactions in Hispanic cultures.

Receptive Skills: Listening and Reading

Recent methodologies and research into second-language acquisition are promoting renewed emphasis on the receptive skills. Typically, these skills have received only secondary consideration in foreign language classes. The availability of authentic printed material and audio- and videotapes of radio and television broadcasts in other languages is growing rapidly. Language as it is spoken and understood by native speakers is the best possible resource for students. What is needed now are activities designed around such materials, as well as guidelines and instruction to help teachers design their own materials.

At the skill-getting stage, students can learn to control language at the discrimination level. As students study grammar or vocabulary, they should be trained to discriminate the sounds and to assign meaning to the pieces of language.

Exercises in listening for discrimination may involve such activities as listening for cues to gender, number, or tense. Focused listening exercises direct the student to pull specific information from a stream of speech. When studying weather, for example, students might listen to a broadcast where several cities are mentioned; they are asked to match the appropriate symbol (for cloudy,

---

9. Seelye, H. Ned, *Teaching Culture: Strategies for Intercultural Communication* (Lincolnwood, Illinois: National Textbook Company, 1984).

sunny, windy, raining) with the city. The key concept is that aural comprehension is assessed without requiring the student to produce language, either in speech or writing. This constraint assures that an inability to speak or write does not interfere with evidence of the students' comprehension.

After the first year of instruction, students should be building the listening skill by practice with paragraph-length segments. Prelistening activities, which help students develop expectations about what they will hear by focusing their attention on general content and key words, contribute to their successful comprehension. During the learning stage, repetition of the selections should be permitted. We cannot assume that listening skills are keen in the first language or that students' listening strategies are efficient. Consequently, teachers must attend both to the general process of listening comprehension and to comprehension in the foreign language.

Our ideas about foreign language reading have changed a great deal in the past decade. Audiolingualism dealt sparingly with methods for teaching reading. It was assumed that students literate in their first language would automatically transfer to reading what they were learning orally in the second language. This approach was severely limiting to students, for it kept their receptive skills from developing as quickly as they might have.

Currently, a few textbooks promote more effective reading by providing word-study exercises, comprehension exercises, and reading hints addressed to the student. Most books, however, consist of passages whose content may appeal to students, but which have no instructional dimension other than a glossary for the vocabulary and questions for comprehension at the end. It is up to the teacher to supply the skill-building dimension.

Teachers can learn to adapt listening and reading selections by building a lesson plan around materials provided in the text. Let us consider the following model, designed by June Phillips:[10]

1. *Preparation.* The purpose of this stage is to give students the general knowledge they will need to understand a passage. Crit-

10. June K. Phillips, "Practical Implications of Recent Research in Reading," *Foreign Language Annals* 17 (1984): 285–296.

ical vocabulary might be taught or reviewed; expectations might be highlighted so that students are alert and their attention focused on the material; cultural background necessary for understanding should be explained. Techniques include brainstorming, interpreting accompanying visual information, predicting the implication of headlines, and reviewing previous information if the passage is a continuation of material students already know.

2. *Skimming/Scanning.* The purpose of this stage is to give students a general idea of a passage before asking them to deal with it in detail. If students have the general picture, they will be less tempted to resort to the slow, word-by-word decoding that characterizes so much foreign language reading. Leading students to move quickly through a passage and helping them grasp general ideas will enhance their contextual guessing and interpretation of meaning in the selection. Techniques include posing a few general questions to be answered in English or the target language, selecting the main idea from a multiple-choice item, underlining topic sentences in reading, and filling in charts for specific information.

3. *Decoding/Detail.* This is the stage at which the teacher guides learners through the language that is just at or beyond the point of fluent comprehension. Decoding is always a fallback strategy for the learner. As long as comprehension is taking place easily, students hear and read on the level of ideas; when unfamiliar words or structures interfere with that progress, they pay conscious attention to the meaning carried by a word or phrase. The teacher may assist the process by checking on the meaning of words or ideas as well as providing cues for useful guessing strategies. Techniques include glosses or word lists, open-ended study questions to lead the student, and actual explication of words or ideas.

4. *Comprehension.* This is the final stage, when the teacher checks that students have really understood what they have read. For evaluation purposes, students should be asked to indicate what they have understood without their having to supply written answers in the foreign language. The comprehension exercises and questions can relate to facts, inferences, and judgments.

Possible formats include true or false, multiple-choice, matching, completion, fill-ins, and summaries.

5. *Transferable or Integrative Skills.* Long after the content of a passage has been forgotten, what the student has learned about how to listen and read should remain. At various points special transfer exercises might be developed to promote effective interpretive skills. These include cognate pattern recognition, word-family study, and practice in guessing from context. Another valuable follow-up for many receptive activities is to use the material that has been read or heard as a point of departure for productive practice.

Productive Skills: Speaking and Writing

Although there is a consensus among language teachers about *how* to teach speaking and writing skills, there are disagreements about *when* to teach these productive skills. Some research suggests that it is better to establish a strong receptive basis in the mind and experience of students before asking them to produce speech. On the other hand, other researchers and teachers are convinced that opportunities for self-expression from the beginning contribute greatly to foreign language proficiency. The fact is that we simply do not know which approach is more effective or, indeed, whether it can be said that one way is superior in all situations with all types of students. Students have succeeded under both of these diametrically opposed approaches. Perhaps this is because of the techniques used to teach the productive skills, no matter when they are introduced in a language program.

Most of the practices designed to teach speaking and writing apply directly to the desired Green Book outcomes for foreign language. These goals suggest that students in the standard sequence develop control of productive language so that they are able (1) to convey personal or biographical information, (2) to converse about interests and their immediate environment, and (3) to manage to survive linguistically in the target culture. At the higher levels the quality and quantity of language produced improve greatly, although the tasks under student control are essentially the same. Our discussion of teaching productive skills will focus on these three areas at the basic and the advanced levels.

Conveying Personal Information:
Personalized Speech and Writing

The formats of exercises described above in the Vocabulary section also apply to speaking and writing in the larger sense. Procedures that guide students from phrases to sentences to paragraphs are best for building proficiency. Most textbook chapters or lesson topics focus on themes that lend themselves to personalization. Omaggio outlines four types of personalized exercises that encourage personal expression:[11]

1. *Personalized questions* are directed to students as real people so that they may respond truthfully. In addition to the format where the teacher asks the question and the student responds, such exercises can be done in student pairs or as small-group activities. Personalized questions often appear in newer texts and can easily be expanded by teachers alert to their students' interests and life-styles.

2. *Personalized completions* resemble the open-ended affective activities described in the Vocabulary section. Examples in German using reflexive verbs follow:

Ich mußte mich beeilen, weil . . . (I had to hurry because . . .)
(I was in a rush because . . .)
Ich habe mich geärgert, weil . . . (I was annoyed because . . .)
Ich habe mich verlaufen, weil . . . (I lost my way because . . .)
(I got lost because . . .)

Students may answer orally or in writing and may be asked to provide multiple answers. Paragraph-length completions are another possibility:

At my house. Complete the following paragraph to describe your house and family.[12]

---

11. Alice C. Omaggio, "The Proficiency-Oriented Classroom," *Teaching for Proficiency: The Organizing Principle*, ed. Theodore V. Higgs (Lincolnwood, Illinois: National Textbook Company, 1984), pp. 60–63.

12. From Rochester, Myrna, Judith Muyskens, Alice C. Omaggio, and Claudene Chalmers, *Bonjour, ça va* (New York: Random House, 1983, p. 114), cited by Alice C. Omaggio, in *Language in Education: Theory and Practice* (Arlington, Virginia: Center for Applied Linguistics, 1979), p. 61.

The room that I prefer is _____ because _____. I spend a lot of time in _____ because _____. I feel very calm in _____ and I study in _____ because _____. I eat in _____ and I have a phone in _____. My family spends a lot of time in _____ because _____.

3. *Sentence builders* require students to choose and connect phrases to express their own ideas. This practice allows for communication with correct structures and assures accuracy.

Weekends	I	hate/s	to sleep
Mondays	my friends	love/s	to read the comics
At night	my teacher	want/s	to get up
Sunday mornings	my family	has/have	to go to church

4. *Personalized true/false exercises*, sometimes called agree/disagree exercises, involve a comprehension prerequisite. After reading or hearing the statement, students restate it with their own viewpoint. Some items concerning school life that have carryover possibilities for real conversation might be the following:

This school is boring.

I love the cafeteria food.

Our teachers are great.

Exams are necessary.

Conversation Skills

The Green Book outcomes specify as goals the ability to maintain a simple conversation and to write a short paragraph on a familiar topic. These parallel expectations for oral and written work mean that the two skills can be smoothly integrated in the classroom. Teachers may prefer to have students prepare a topic in writing before speaking about it. Sometimes it works better to have the written assignment follow the oral presentation. Since conversation means speaking spontaneously, without preparation or memorization, students must be given practice in developing this ability.

As teachers know, conversation practice in the classroom is hard to organize well. The chief problems are the maintenance of discipline, teacher supervision of the activity, and evaluation. Many teachers reject out of hand the idea of using small-group activities, but this technique can be very productive once teachers learn how to manage such groups. The advantage of small groups, of course, is that students get more time to talk and more practice with many conversational formats. Teachers will profit by acquainting themselves with the literature on small-group instructional techniques. A few guidelines especially effective for foreign language classes are the following:

1. Have students work in pairs or threes rather than in larger groups. This parallels conversational numbers and keeps the participation at a maximum for each student.

2. Assign short, narrowly structured tasks at the beginning. As students become adept at working in small groups, the time and complexity can be expanded because the process will be familiar.

3. Even though the real goal for each activity is speech, try to create a product for each small group, something to be turned in. This might take the form of "minutes" or notes on what happened, a check sheet on the content of the interaction, or even an actual tape of the conversation if that is practical. This leads students to be disciplined in following instructions, since they know their work will be checked.

If students are to develop conversational skills, they must practice conversing in virtually every unit of study. Most text chapters lend themselves quite well to questions that promote conversation. The teacher may wish to go over these questions with the full class, but students also need practice in asking, as well as answering, questions.

Small-group work lends itself well to practice in asking questions. One controlled technique for guiding students as they assume leadership for maintaining conversation is the use of Conversation and Interview Cards.[13] The students work in pairs; each student is given a card with a series of questions to pose to a partner. They should be encouraged to expand the conversation with a few additional original queries. If a third person is added, he or she assumes the

13. Therese Bonin and Diane Birckbichler, "Real Communication through Conversation and Interview Cards," *Modern Language Journal* 59 (1975): 22–25.

role of monitor. Equipped with a card that provides answers, or suggested ones, the monitor acts as an evaluator and a control. Roles can rotate so that each student has an opportunity to ask, to answer, and to verify. Here is an example on the topic of careers.

Card 1: Ask your partner
- what he or she wants to do
- why he or she chooses that career
- what training or education is required
- what he or she would hate to do

Card 2: Ask your partner
- what one of his or her relatives does
- where this relative works
- what the hours are
- what advantages or disadvantages the job has

Throughout the course the teacher should assess the students' progress in conversational ability by leading small groups (three to five students) through some review and newer topics, using an interview format. While class size may prevent this from being done as often as one might like, even a few times a year benefits students and gives them a dose of individual attention that increases motivation. The rest of the class will need to be kept busy during these small-group interviews; a composition or a reading assignment might fill that need, as would any of the "seat work" strategies devised by elementary school teachers. Interviewing in small groups also has the advantage of reducing pressure some students experience, since no student has to answer every question. Before meeting with a group, the teacher should draw up a guide list of questions in three categories: (1) a few warm-up questions to put students at ease, to review familiar topics, and to stimulate conversation; (2) questions focused on newer materials at the core of the current instruction; (3) a few natural wind-down questions to send students off with a feeling of accomplishment. Evaluation is probably best achieved with a global rating based on success of communication, accuracy of structure given the level of the students, pronunciation, and so forth.

Appropriate topics for students attempting to achieve the basic outcomes include

- Social niceties (greetings, leave-takings, introductions)
- Identification (address, nationality, age or date of birth, occupation)
- Descriptions (family members, occupation, residence; home environment; school and courses; possessions and objects; likes and dislikes; activities, pastimes, job, entertainment; friends)

More advanced students should also be able to

- Express feelings (about events, people)
- Discuss past events and future plans
- Ask for, refuse, accept dates and invitations
- Make small talk
- Make appointments
- Behave with greater cultural appropriateness in a range of situations

Written tasks may follow similar procedures. Letter-writing formats are particularly realistic. Students may correspond on topics of interest and everyday life. They may also write short compositions on a given topic, or even poems. Writing assignments can also be a part of small-group activities; one student acts as recorder of the oral discussion and turns in a written account of the activity.

Survival and Everyday Living Skills

Conversational ability concerns living skills in the other language. This type of activity does not depend only on travel to other countries, a possibility not open to all students. Many languages are spoken widely in this country; many foreign visitors would benefit from the help a foreign language student might provide. We are interested in the ability to obtain shelter, food, and transportation and to shop for oneself or others. Effective classroom procedures involve role playing or problem solving. Instructions, again, can be given on index cards, which are selected by students or groups of students at appropriate times in the course. They then act out the situation to see how they can "survive" linguistically. The same cards, or ones with slight variations, can be used throughout a sequence of courses, for the situation differs less than does the ability with which it is carried out.

Simple situation: Shopping. Go into a store and ask:
- what fruits are a good buy today
- how much they cost
- for the number of fruits you want
- whether the merchant sells bread as well
- whether you can have a bag for your purchase

Complicated situation: Shopping. Go into a store and say:
- you bought a dozen oranges yesterday
- when you cut them open they were rotten
- they tasted awful
- you are returning eight of them
- you want your money refunded

Some everyday topics at the basic level include simple situations:

- Getting around (asking for directions, understanding the response)
- Using the post office, airport, public transportation, banks
- Getting food (understanding menus, ordering, paying, tipping)
- Shopping (where, how to buy, quantities, money systems)
- Getting a room (hotel, youth hostel, dormitory)
- Meeting emergency needs (health, forms, telephone, finances)
- Helping foreign speakers in the United States (socializing, helping at school or work, volunteering)

For more advanced students these situations may involve less-common routines and may contain complications:

- Dealing with the unexpected (lost luggage, missed planes, theft, finances, health, accidents)
- Complaining (food, lodging, courses, communications)
- Obtaining personal services (barber, cleaner, laundromat, car repair)
- Giving directions to someone here or in another country
- Sustaining social conversation and interacting with people on a daily basis

Role playing often has an unexpected appeal for the least likely members of the class. Very often the shy student responds actively to this device; creative students have a chance to use positive cognitive skills even though their language may be limited. Usually students enjoy the activity, and it proves to them how much they can finally do with language. It is a chance to perform, an opportunity often denied in foreign language classes, although in other disciplines such as art or music a student would not be asked to practice without the reward of performance always ahead.

Conclusion

This chapter has presented some ideas for achieving specific instructional goals. Realizing that many teachers who read this book will have district curriculum guides that are heavily grammar-based and oriented toward the textbook, we have tried to suggest ways in which teachers might revise their classroom activities toward realistic communication and language proficiency.

While the activities described in this chapter are designed to improve students' proficiency in a foreign language, they also contribute to the development of Basic Academic Competencies. Chapter 5 deals with the contribution of foreign language study to students' general education.

V. Foreign Language and the Basic Academic Competencies

The typical high school schedule divides a student's day into segments devoted to English, history, science, foreign language, and so forth. For each course students have separate textbooks, notebooks, homework assignments, and tests. They come to think, and justifiably so, that their courses are discrete, unrelated activities.

The truth is that students' academic subjects are linked by general competencies common to all of them. *Academic Preparation for College* names the following Basic Academic Competencies: reading, writing, speaking and listening, mathematics, reasoning, studying, using computers, and observing. These competencies are the tools that students bring with them to their academic courses to enable them to understand and use the material of those courses. In turn, these competencies are also the broad intellectual skills that are developed by the academic course work; students take these skills with them as they go on to more advanced work in college.

This chapter treats the connections between foreign language and the Basic Academic Competencies. Our approach is to accompany the reader on a visit to the foreign language classes of an imaginary high school in a city in Florida. As we look in on classes in a variety of languages at different levels, we can see the ways in which students are building their basic skills while they are engaged in a foreign language lesson.

Reading

A European Disneyland

The scene is Mr. Romero's third-year Spanish class. The students are reading an article from the international edition of the Spanish newspaper El País. *As we look in, Mr. Romero is leading the class in prereading exercises. For the reading lesson he has chosen an article on negotiations between Walt Disney Productions and the Spanish government for a European Disneyland park. Disney World is close enough to the school that all of the students have been there, and many of them know it well. Some even have family members who work at the park.*

Mr. Romero's first step is to pass out copies of the article and to ask (in Spanish, of course): "What is this? A page from a novel? An advertisement?"

Student: "It's from a newspaper."

Mr. Romero: "How do you know?"

Student: "It looks like a newspaper. It has a title in big letters."

Mr. Romero: "Where was it written?"

Student: "In Spain. Barcelona."

Mr. Romero: "How do you know?"

Student: "It says Barcelona in small letters at the top."

And so the discussion continues. After it has been established that this is an article from a Spanish newspaper, Mr. Romero has the students scan the article quickly (for about a minute), underlining words they know. Students call out words, and Mr. Romero writes them on the blackboard. The list is heavy on cognates and English words: Walt Disney Productions, Disneylandia, Europa, España, Francia, Paris, *2,000 millones de dólares, parque, gobierno, negociaciones.* Mr. Romero has the students silently read the headline, the first sentence, and the list of known words and then asks for guesses about the topic of the article. Students quickly come to the conclusion that it has something to do with building a park like Disney World in Spain or France.

Mr. Romero continues with the reading lesson. The students have gone through a process that is often automatic for first-language readers who pick up a newspaper or a magazine: before they start to read, they figure out what kind of text they are reading and what the topic is. With that information behind them, they can begin to read with accurate expectations of what they will encounter.

The time-honored method of guiding students through a foreign language text consists of having them answer discrete-point questions that the teacher prepares beforehand about specific words or details of the content. This process is based on the assumption that the comprehension of each individual word is equivalent to an understanding of the text as a whole. It also links the students' understanding of a written work very closely to that of the teacher, since the students learn to rely heavily on the teacher's interpretive questions as they read. A look at the Basic Academic Competency in reading, however, suggests that we want to aim for more direct interaction between the students, the text, and the author. The reading competency includes the abilities to identify and comprehend the main and subordinate ideas in a written work, to identify a writer's point of view and tone, and to vary one's reading speed and method. The approach that Mr. Romero has used will help students progress to the point in foreign language reading where they can confront a text without reliance on "comprehension" questions, glossed vocabulary, and simplified syntax.

What questions can teachers ask students to guide them in understanding a text—that is, questions that are not of the discrete-point where-when-who-what variety? Janet K. Swaffar discusses four types of questions or assignments that help students identify the organizational strategies writers themselves use.[1] By seeing how the author has organized the text, students can grasp its meaning in a deeper way than a word-for-word translation could accomplish. These assignments might include having the students (1) find the places where the author mentions events that happened in the past; (2) sequence the events in the text in the order in which they are mentioned; (3) discover the various ways in which the author refers to the same person or event; and (4) look for the causes of events mentioned in the text.

The best foreign language reader is the one who recognizes cognate patterns and word families, guesses sensibly from context, takes advantage of format and other visual cues, and looks up words accurately. These abilities receive extensive practice in all foreign language courses.

Foreign language teachers often have an advantage over their native-language colleagues when it comes to teaching reading: since their students are beginners, nothing is taken for granted. Teachers can address the real issues of comprehension by using simple texts

---

1. Janet K. Swaffar, "Reading Authentic Texts in a Foreign Language: A Cognitive Model," *Modern Language Journal* 69 (Spring 1985): 15–34.

and can help students to see that all language, no matter how straightforward, communicates more than a literal message. Consequently, foreign language learners have ample opportunity to improve these skills and can carry them over into the native language, whether consciously or unconsciously.

Writing

The foreign language class can provide ample opportunity to develop writing skills: the students are guided through the process of focusing on the word, the sentence, and the paragraph. Writing in a foreign language not only improves communication and proficiency in that language, but also increases students' literacy in English. The "process approach" to writing, a method by which students revise and improve their writing assignments through several drafts, has the additional advantage of demonstrating that the production of good writing involves an investment of time and hard work.

German Pen Pals

The scene is Mr. Krauss's second-year German class. Several years ago, through a notice in a professional journal, he discovered a teacher in a secondary school in Bonn who was interested in establishing ties with a "sister class" in the United States. Mr. Krauss has asked his students to write as a homework assignment the first letter of the year to their German pen pals. The writing task is authentic in that he has created a situation in which students communicate information about themselves to real people with whom they are establishing a relationship.

Mr. Krauss's writing project has the additional special feature of being bilingual. The students write to each other once a month, alternating between German and English. Mr. Krauss has the students engage in the same process of analyzing, editing, and rewriting their drafts in both languages, in the belief that writing skills can be developed in, and applied to, both English and German. The letters in the native language are, of course, longer and more complex, and Mr. Krauss takes care to assign writing tasks and topics for each letter that are appropriate for the students' different levels of proficiency in the two languages.

The students analyze not only their own letters but also those of their German pen pals. In this particular class, Mr. Krauss displays on the overhead projector a letter in German from a student in the Bonn class. The student had written about a trip she took with her family to visit her grandparents in a rural section of southern Germany. In the letter she compared the physical and social features of the rural area with those of the capital city of Bonn, and reflected on the different values and life-styles of teenagers living in the country and in the city. When Mr. Krauss has the students read the letter, he uses many of the same reading comprehension techniques that Mr. Romero used with the newspaper article.

Once the students understand the content of the letter, they and Mr. Krauss discuss the organization of ideas and the writing style. He asks for observations about the following points:

1. What information is presented (first, second, last)
2. Whether there is a clearly stated main idea in each paragraph
3. The general tone of the letter
4. The writer's point of view about life in the country and life in the city
5. How the writer handles transitions from one idea to another

Through the active participation of the students, Mr. Krauss is providing the class with some basic tools needed for the letters they themselves write.

He has the students write their own letters on mimeographs so that he can make copies for everyone in the class. Students have brought in their first drafts, and all students have a packet of 25 letters in which they describe their house, their neighborhood, or their city. The students have been told to include short introductory and final paragraphs and to devote one paragraph to the main description.

At this point Mr. Krauss is ready to start the process of editing, revising, and rewriting. He divides the class of 25 students into 5 groups. The students in each group will read and discuss one another's letters, giving suggestions to improve the organization of ideas, choice of words, and grammar. Mr. Krauss will select one letter from each group and, using the overhead projector, will invite the class to offer other suggestions for improvement. By having the students phrase their comments in the form of "suggestions for improvement," Mr. Krauss is subtly training students to make constructive criticism in a skillful and tactful way while also allowing them to practice listening and speaking skills.

Rewriting assignments is an important part of learning how to write well and will give the students confidence in their ability to solve problems in their writing. Students need to experience writing as a process of devoting themselves to clear thinking and improved communication. In rewriting they develop alternatives after weaknesses are pointed out. They work their own transformations of grammar and learn to resolve difficulties by using reference tools at their command, like dictionaries and grammar books. They practice the art of finding meaning and of expressing their thoughts in a lucid and correct form. Since the task of writing demands a knowledge of basic grammar, the students realize the need for it.

Mr. Krauss has found that class editing has important benefits for students:

1. Their efforts to improve the work of their friends and classmates improves their attention in class.
2. By their efforts to vary sentence structure and word choice within a paragraph, they learn additional vocabulary items and syntactic forms.
3. They become aware of the impact of good writing on the reader.
4. They learn how to criticize their own writing and to pay greater attention to detail.

Writing is communication. In Mr. Krauss's class the writing is intended for a real audience—the German pen pals. The students' desire to "write it like it is" is enhanced, since they know that real responses from real readers are forthcoming. In addition, the collaboration among students fosters a spirit of cooperation that works for the benefit of all.

Speaking and Listening

The art of communication effectively involves two basic skills that are often taken for granted in one's native language, speaking and listening. Nevertheless, many students come to high school with an inability to answer or ask questions coherently or to follow simple instructions. Their questions and answers are punctuated with frequent phrases such as "You know what I mean?" Many students seem to have difficulty grasping information that is delivered orally. Because students have to go back to the fundamentals of communication when they begin foreign language study, the foreign language classroom is a good place to give students practice in basic communication skills that they may not have developed and used in their native language. Carefully planned small-group activities can help students develop clarity of expression, which depends on careful listening and processing of information.

Clothes Make the (Wo)man

We look in on Ms. Rivier's first-year French class, which is involved in a small-group exercise to give students an opportunity to ask and answer questions about articles of clothing.[2] The core vocabulary list from their text has already been expanded to include items of clothing that the students wanted to be able to discuss. The class has been divided into groups of three, and each group has a copy of the checklist.

Nom (Name): _____

Portes-tu . . . ? (Do you wear . . . ?)	*toujours* (always)	*parfois* (sometimes)	*jamais* (never)
des bluejeans (jeans)	_____	_____	_____
une cravate (tie)	_____	_____	_____
une jupe (skirt)	_____	_____	_____
un anorak (ski jacket)	_____	_____	_____
une chemise (shirt)	_____	_____	_____
des pantalons (pants)	_____	_____	_____
une ceinture (belt)	_____	_____	_____
des chaussures de tennis (sneakers)	_____	_____	_____
une casquette (cap)	_____	_____	_____

2. The example is taken from an exercise created by Leah Chiambalero, Mary Ellen Logan, Edward Ray, and Carolyn Staton at the ACTFL-sponsored National Endowment for the Humanities Summer Proficiency Institute, Haverford College, Haverford, Pennsylvania, July 1983.

The exercise has several purposes: (1) to practice new vocabulary in a personally relevant and communicative context; (2) to practice asking questions in French; (3) to practice taking turns in conversation; (4) to practice listening and speaking skills.

Using the model suggested by the checklist, Jeanne asks Monique a question: "Portes-tu des bluejeans?" to which Monique responds: "Oui, toujours" or "Je porte toujours des bluejeans." Since this exchange simulates real conversation, there is no requirement that students answer with complete sentences; the only requirement is that they convey comprehensibly the requested information. Jeanne then continues with more questions: "Portes-tu une cravate?" Monique answers: "Je ne porte jamais de cravate." While this interaction is going on between the two students, Jacques listens and marks the checklist. It will look something like this at the end of the exchange:

Nom (Name): _____

Portes-tu . . . ? (Do you wear . . . ?)	*toujours* (always)	*parfois* (sometimes)	*jamais* (never)
des bluejeans (jeans)	X		
une cravate (tie)			X
une jupe (skirt)		X	
un anorak (ski jacket)		X	
une chemise (shirt)		X	
des pantalons (pants)		X	
une ceinture (belt)			X
des chaussures de tennis (sneakers)	X		
une casquette (cap)			X

Once the answers have been recorded, Jacques reports to the class: "Monique porte toujours des bluejeans. Monique ne porte jamais de cravate. Elle porte parfois une jupe." And so on. Although this is not conversation in the true sense because it is based almost exclusively on patterns, the exercise does provide for communication among the students in contrast with the more traditional exercise, in which the teacher asks most of the questions and the students answer. Here the students are experiencing language as communication and are able to use their limited vocabulary and grammatical resources to exchange authentic personal information.

Ms. Rivier's exercise gives listening as important a role as speaking. Students often have trouble focusing their attention in class when they are part of a large group. The small group and the focused oral exchange make it easier for the listener (Jacques in this example) to concentrate on the most important information. The listener also has the responsibility of noting down and then reporting the information, which increases the motivation for paying close attention to what is going on.

Although students in a first-year language class are still far from the level of proficiency in listening comprehension and speaking that is described by the foreign language learning outcomes, activities like the one described above allow them to develop the oral skills they need to become successful communicators later on. In an elementary fashion, the students in class are developing a basic academic competence in the ability to answer and ask questions concisely and to follow spoken instructions. The step-by-step process not only has value in second-language learning, but applies to the native language as well.

Reasoning

The reasoning skill—the ability to perceive the different parts that make a whole and how they interrelate—provides a necessary basis for developing many other skills. The study of Latin contributes to the development of reasoning skills in many ways. The following example illustrates one way in which the study of the Latin language provides a unique vantage point for the development of basic reasoning skill.

Word Power

The scene is Ms. Ellison's first-year Latin class. The students are working on simple sentences that consist of subject, verb, and object. The elements of Latin grammar they are using are the nominative and the accusative cases of nouns and the present tense of verbs. Ms. Ellison writes the same sentence on the blackboard in three different ways:

Marcus epistolam scribit.

Epistolam Marcus scribit.

Scribit Marcus epistolam.

Students are asked to identify the subject, verb, and object in the three sentences. They have little difficulty with the first sentence, although, unlike in English, the direct object precedes the verb. In the second sentence, however, they must resist the strongly ingrained tendency of native speakers of English to identify the first word in the sentence as the subject. Ms. Ellison makes use of the careful attention to the endings in order to complete the task and make her point.

The students are led to see that, unlike in English, word order does not determine the function a word plays in the Latin sentence. In English the subject is determined by its coming first in the sentence, but in Latin a -us ending can mark a subject. While the English direct object follows a verb, the Latin direct object can be indicated by an -m ending. A singular subject requires a -t verb ending. When Ms. Ellison later presents students with the sentence "Amici epistolam scribunt," they know the subject is plural, given the -nt verb ending.

The way Latin signals word function so differently from English leads students to examine more closely how their own language operates. The nature of the Latin system of morphology and syntax enables students to develop a clearer concept of linguistic features; this becomes more evident as the complexity of the Latin sentence increases. For example, the sentence "Marcus epistolam puellae scribit" illustrates how students must be able to combine information about morphology—namely, that "puellae" could be any of three different forms—with information about syntax—namely, that "Marcus epistolam" seems to be the subject and object of a transitive active sentence, as well as with information about semantic features—namely, that "scribit" is like certain other verbs of "giving and telling" that often occur with a dative. In analyzing the sentence, the student must reject "puellae" as nominative plural because "Marcus" can only be nominative singular, and there is no connection between them that would allow both to be subjects. In addition, the verb morphology shows agreement with a singular subject. The reasoning involved in rejecting "puellae" as genitive is more difficult, since a genitive is always possible if there is a noun-head to be modified. In this sentence, the semantic features of "scribit" point to an indirect object interpretation. Ms. Ellison also makes use of the vocabulary in the Latin sentence to help the students think about English vocabulary: "epistolam"—epistle, epistolary; "scribit"—scribe, enscribe, scripture.

Thus, the reasoning skills so important for understanding the structure of the Latin sentence may be used to increase students' sensitivity to the structure of their native language. This, in turn, makes for better reading and writing. Operating by analogy, the teacher may use the vocabulary presented in the Latin class to enlarge the students' English vocabulary.

Culture and the Observing Competency

Foreign language study offers students an excellent opportunity to become observers of other cultures and, at the same time, to become culturally aware of their own surroundings. Most students come to high school with a limited knowledge of other cultures, most often derived from an accumulation of facts presented in isolation or from stereotypical ideas presented through the media.[3]

All Americans Are Rich

In her French class Ms. Demarest integrates the learning of language and culture in a process that will ultimately result in a Green Book basic learning outcome: the ability to see and to interpret things and events in the social environment and to record such observations in appropriate form. *For her lesson on culture and stereotyping, Ms. Demarest has compiled a variety of audiovisuals that depict French people. She brings to class magazine pictures, a videotape provided by a local travel agency, several posters and*

---

3. The example in this section was inspired by a presentation by Wendy W. Allen, "Involvement and Commitment through Culture/Civilization Courses," ACTFL Annual Meeting, New York, November 1983.

newspaper ads printed by airlines, as well as other advertisements for a French bakery, a French restaurant, and the like. All these have been produced with American viewers and consumers in mind. She also has asked her students to scan local newspapers and magazines for additional ads. By making her students active participants in the project, she has not only generated interest on the part of her students but has also begun the process of initiating them into becoming discerning observers and interpreters of visual materials. *One student has brought an ad for a French perfume, another an ad for French jeans, and so on.*

Since this is a beginning class, the dialogue between teacher and students is in English. (For more advanced classes, she switches to French.) Ms. Demarest asks the students to take a piece of paper; as she shows the students each one of the pictures, she asks them to observe carefully and to write down the salient characteristics of each scene. After showing the last of the visuals, she asks the students to read aloud what they have written. Their lists look something like this:

1. French women are very sexy.
2. The French use a lot of perfume because they are so romantic.
3. French men always wear berets.
4. The favorite pastime for the French is drinking wine in sidewalk cafes.
5. French people are best known for their joviality (joie de vivre).
6. French schoolchildren wear shorts and carry their books in satchels.

The list goes on, depending on the students' views, but Ms. Demarest does not immediately point out that their observations are based on stereotypes created by the media. Instead, she moves on to the second part of the assignment and shows pictures and advertisements made in France that involve the stereotypical French view of Americans. The students are now asked to write down the characteristics of Americans as they would be perceived through French eyes. Their lists look like this:

1. Americans eat only hamburgers and fast food.
2. All Americans are rich.
3. All Americans have two cars and houses in the suburbs with swimming pools.

4. Americans love to chew gum.
5. All Americans wear cowboy boots.

Ms. Demarest then asks the students to read their lists and encourages them to react critically to their own observations. While at first the students may not have been aware of the stereotypical presentations in the French visuals, they will detect stereotyping in the second part of the assignment.

From the initial perceptions and reactions to the cultural phenomena, Ms. Demarest has the students pursue different aspects of the theme of stereotyping by describing and analyzing their original perceptions and by comparing both the target and the native cultures. In her dialogue with the students, Ms. Demarest uses a question-and-answer technique to elicit responses. She asks, "What did you first see in the photographs and slides?" Then she says, "Let's look at them individually. What do they tell us about the French? About ourselves?" Another question is "What are your reactions?"

Through the questioning technique Ms. Demarest has initiated her students into a learning process that will ultimately teach them how to *perceive* with a more critical viewpoint and to recognize that we see through the filter of our culture and experiences. Once the students have had an opportunity to express their perceptions, they move to another stage of cultural awareness where they might relate how their perceptions changed in the process. They can respond to questions in a broader context, such as "Why are there cultural differences?" "What effects have geography, time, and people had on cultural evolution?" "What differences exist between the two cultures?" "Are there any influences of the target culture on the native culture?" "Has the native culture influenced the target culture in any way?" "If your cultural perceptions changed during this unit, what caused them to change?"[4]

Learning about the culture of the target language has traditionally been a part of the curriculum of foreign language courses. Sometimes these lessons are presented as culture capsules, culture clusters, cultural minidramas, and the like. The assumption is that the

---

4. Linda M. Crawford-Lange, "Doing the Unthinkable in the Second-Language Classroom: A Process for the Integration of Language and Culture," in *Teaching for Proficiency: The Organizing Principle*, ed. Theodore V. Higgs, p. 149.

culture is a separate, optional entity, essentially informational, for enrichment. The Basic Academic Competencies suggest, however, that the culture be integrated with language learning so that students may *understand the close connection between language and thought* and *become aware of the cultural diversity among the peoples of the world.* It is therefore a *process* rather than an accumulation of facts or informational bits. Linda M. Crawford-Lange and Dale L. Lange offer an integrative process that includes eight stages: (1) identification of a cultural theme, (2) presentation of cultural phenomena, (3) dialogue in either target or native language, (4) transition to language learning, (5) language learning, (6) verification of perceptions, (7) cultural awareness, and (8) evaluation of language and cultural proficiency.[5] The stages, which take students from learning about a topic of interest to them to exploring the cultural features of the topic to the teacher's evaluation of their cultural proficiency, provide interesting and natural ways to integrate culture and language in the classroom.

Studying

Learning a foreign language requires a set of study skills ranging from simple rote memorization to problem solving. These skills are essential to "learning how to learn," and no efficient work in foreign language can be done without them. Basic to all these skills is the ability to listen, which students must understand is *not* a passive activity. Students then must set goals and priorities, short- and long-term, according to the course objectives, and establish the proper environment for managing their studies. They learn quickly that to acquire proficiency in a foreign language, they must set up a routine for doing, reviewing, and practicing the daily assignments, which are an integral part of the cumulative aspect of foreign language learning. Teachers can help students see the need to

---

5. Linda M. Crawford-Lange and Dale L. Lange, "Doing the Unthinkable in the Second-Language Classroom: A Process for the Integration of Language and Culture," in *Teaching for Proficiency: The Organizing Principle*, ed. Theodore V. Higgs, pp. 139-177.

improve their skills by discussing time allotments, study surroundings, and specific methods that will work well for them, both in and out of school. Few courses in the curriculum demand the time and energy every day that a foreign language class does. Review and practice of the work students have done will make them see the importance of the building blocks of language skills. All they have done before is necessary to what they will learn later.

The foreign language class can provide opportunities for students to develop skills in using outside resources such as libraries, computers, and people in the community, and to blend knowledge from these sources into their learning strategies. Students might talk with people in their neighborhoods who speak the language they are studying, gather written materials in the foreign language, watch foreign language programs on television, or go to foreign films. In regions where the foreign language is used extensively in the community, students can be encouraged to carry out assignments "in place," such as interviewing community leaders or observing and then describing the routines of an ethnic community.

A comment heard often from students who take a foreign language is that they learn as much about their native language as they do about the foreign language they are studying. The possibilities for expanding students' native vocabulary in both general and specialized areas are obvious (as is getting a firmer grasp on the structures and subtleties of the native language). Students develop and use these vocabularies in the four basic skills and in computing and studying. The Romance languages and Latin, especially, provide a wide range of vocabulary opportunities for students. New words learned through the foreign language are often related to "formal" English words. From basic words such as *flood, hand, food,* and *lawyer* will come *inundate, manual, nourishment,* and *advocate.* Students with a weak first-language vocabulary can enrich it by foreign language study; those with a good knowledge of English vocabulary will enliven it.

Many terms learned in foreign language classes are found in other disciplines as well: the elements and their abbreviations in chemistry (Fe—*fer;* Ag—*argent;* Pb—*plomb;* Cu—*cuivre);* terms in economics and history *(laissez-faire, coup d'état, bourgeoisie, nouveau riche);* food and cooking terms *(cuisine, croissant, Wiener schnitzel, enchiladas);* terms in psychology and philosophy *(Angst, Weltsch-*

merz). These and many others allow foreign language learners to make new connections using "old" knowledge.

Especially at the intermediate and advanced levels of language learning, students must be able to recall, understand, analyze, summarize, and report the main ideas gleaned from readings, lectures, and discussions. They must synthesize these skills and apply them to new situations. As more effort is made to develop the receptive skills at every level, the cognitive skills will improve. Students can be asked to analyze the motivations of a character in a novel or a play, or to summarize the events of a chapter or a scene; to report orally or in writing the main points of a lecture or a magazine article, or the consensus of a group discussion.

Students can become relatively effective in devising learning strategies for classwork and for homework. Test-taking strategies require skills of a different kind. Teachers can prepare students for various types of exams—showing them how to pace themselves and which questions to answer or omit, and how to organize, write, and edit a coherent essay within a given time span. For proficiency-based testing, learning and practicing these skills is imperative. Since foreign language study emphasizes the four skills and culture, students must learn to adapt to many assessment devices, some of which are unique to foreign language.

Without the freedom to risk mistakes and to learn from them, students will not venture far beyond the simple repetition of familiar structures. The teacher, experienced in the ways of young people, will make constructive criticism in a skillful and sensitive way. Nothing will be gained by interrupting to correct the pronunciation of a student who is struggling to put together a coherent utterance, or by using more red ink than blue to correct an essay. Students will respond positively to criticism when it is fair, objective, and timely; when it is viewed as a common and necessary enterprise in the classroom; and when it is done with patience, understanding, and good humor.

Mathematics

Some mathematics competencies do have a role to play in foreign language study. For example, it is not unreasonable to expect students to add, subtract, multiply, and divide in the foreign language and to learn the metric system, commonly used all over the world except in the United States. Students need to practice these skills in order to count; give historical and birth dates; use telephone numbers; read train, plane, theater, movie, and TV schedules; tell time using the 24-hour system; make currency exchanges; describe height and weight and clothing sizes—in short, to learn how to make their way in the practical and necessary routines of daily living. Knowledge of these skills is an indispensable part of foreign language instruction. Foreign language study provides ample opportunities for students to become proficient at using the simple arithmetic of everyday life.

Computer Competency

Computers are being touted as the "new technology," in foreign language study as in other academic areas. The potential for computer-assisted instruction is great. The computer is already being used in schools by students and teachers to receive, store, analyze, and interpret information, and as a means of instruction and communication as well. Reviews of computer programs are appearing in the learned journals along with the advertisements of computer manufacturers and distributors. Many programs are already on the market, most involving vocabulary building. But software may be purchased that allows drill in verbs and structure problems ranging from definite articles to possessive pronouns. Other software can open a door to paragraph building, conversation, games, and travel situations. The foreign language student and teacher can do many things at the computer. Drill can be less tedious than when a text or a workbook is used, and the feedback is immediate—and visual. It is, however, important not to be dazzled or disoriented by the possibilities the computer offers. Selection among those possibilities should be guided by the communicative purposes and the proficiency goals of the foreign language curriculum.

Conclusion

The Basic Academic Competencies are common to all academic areas, but are especially pertinent to foreign language because of the added "double dimension" of foreign language study. Learning a foreign language involves more than building vocabulary, using proper verb tenses, or speaking with an "acceptable" pronunciation. It involves learning well the four basic skills—reading, writing, speaking, and listening—and also acquiring the culture of the country whose language is being studied. To acquire the culture of a foreign country inevitably engages the observing and the problem-solving skills that discover diversity to be both interesting and desirable.

VI. Toward Further Discussion

The purpose of this chapter is to look beyond what we have already said about proficiency outcomes and how to achieve them. Many of the questions we have raised in this book remain unanswered. Indeed, our task has been to raise important questions about the teaching of foreign language in secondary schools in a context that will encourage discussion about them.

This is a good time to be a foreign language teacher. There is more interest in our field, both within our own ranks and in the public at large, than there has been for decades. Practical economic needs and educational considerations have led commissions formed by government agencies and private organizations to call for greater emphasis on foreign language and international studies. Within the educational community, the shift toward higher standards and the reestablishment of requirements have favored foreign language departments with increasing enrollments at secondary and postsecondary levels. Satellite communication and video technology have opened new horizons in the preparation of authentic materials from other countries.

Even while foreign language programs in some schools are growing in numbers and in vitality, we should not overlook the difficulties that face language teachers and, to some degree, all teachers. The first and most obvious of these is that a classroom is simply not a good place to learn a language. The enthusiasm and linguistic gain of students who are fortunate enough to spend time in a country where the language is spoken attest to the importance of experiencing language as it is used by native speakers in a variety of settings. Much of what we have written in this book is an attempt to recreate the multidimensional experience of being immersed in the language and culture. The good teacher tries to help students grasp emotionally, as well as intellectually, that the foreign language and its cultures form a constellation of meanings that is as rich and varied as our own. There are those, in addition, who would argue that schools are not particularly conducive to learning. Certainly the segmented time schedule, large classes, and pressures on adolescents to focus on activities other than learning make the task of all teachers a difficult one.

Rather than concentrate on the problems, however, we have tried to focus on directions that teachers can take to help their students learn the fundamentals of a foreign language most effectively. This means that curricula have to be revised, and we have tried in Chapter 3 to outline a process that teachers can follow in making decisions about curricular changes. Many teachers who have learned about proficiency-based outcomes are aware that the curriculum has become too crowded. Teachers are not able to do justice to the content and skills they teach. The result is that while students may have learned many discrete facts about the grammar and vocabulary of a language, they have internalized very little, so that their gain in language proficiency is often minimal.

We would like to invite teachers who are interested in revitalizing high school language programs to join us in a continuing dialogue on the important issues in foreign language teaching. In this chapter we identify and discuss some of the issues we see as important. We recognize, however, that those of you who respond to our invitation to participate in discussion and change will have additional issues for the agenda. Indeed, many unresolved issues are already the focus of conference presentations and journal articles. The Educational EQuality Project is a 10-year effort, and this book represents only one marker along the way. We look forward to discussing with you all issues that you believe to be important. We hope that local discussions will enable groups of teachers to come at least to interim decisions about some of these issues.

How will these discussions take place? This book—like its five companions—can provide one basis for such discussions. The EQuality project intends to organize teacher dialogues around the country, and groups of teachers might organize similar discussions on their own. In-service sessions with small groups of teachers might focus on curriculum design, instructional strategies, or development of supplementary materials. It may prove worthwhile to produce videotapes illustrating the ways in which teachers are building on the suggestions in this book, and to engage with groups of teachers in longer-range projects.

Dealing with Large and Small Classes

Many of the day-to-day problems teachers face relate in some way to class size. In older methods of teaching language, which involved such activities as translation, filling in the blanks, and choral response, class size was not a major issue. With the current emphasis on oral skills and effective communication, class activities now require that students have opportunities for individual practice and for feedback. Class size, therefore, has become a significant element in the planning and carrying out of a language program. Small-group activities are the best way to provide students with more oral practice during the class period; the management of such groups is described in Chapter 4. Even so, the number of small groups that teachers can manage effectively and the amount of time that they can spend with each group are limited.

Ironically, first-year classes, in which students need a great deal of attention, tend to be the largest. Since advanced courses seem to depend on starting with a large group, teachers are understandably reluctant to turn students away from first-year classes. The result in many schools is that overlarge beginning courses exist side by side with extremely small classes in later years.

The administrative solution to the problem of small advanced classes is to combine levels: a teacher might have third- and fourth-year or fourth- and fifth-year students in the same class. This is not a good situation, but teachers have accepted it as a necessary compromise. Workshops at conferences and a growing number of articles in the professional literature are addressing the question of strategies for dealing with this situation. The most successful ones seem to be split periods, independent study, individualized instruction, contract learning, and special-interest minicourses. Clearly, dealing with this difficult situation demands further discussion. Since we know that attaining the Green Book proficiency outcomes takes time, students should have the opportunity to study a language through their senior year of high school. Moreover, the structure of their classes must allow them to practice the skills that constitute the proficiency goals.

Resolving the Content Issue: Grammar, Communication, Literature, Culture

While teachers generally accept proficiency goals for foreign language study, there certainly is no consensus about the type of curriculum that is most likely to promote these outcomes. As discussed in Chapter 3, virtually all textbooks and, therefore, language problems are organized around a succession of grammatical topics. Newer materials combine the grammatical approach with functional, communicative activities directed toward the goal that students should be able to use their knowledge of structure in real conversational language.

Some researchers and teachers are discussing a more radical approach, which would be to place something other than grammar at the center of the curriculum. For example, how would language courses operate if culture were at the center of the curriculum, or if reaching a particular proficiency goal were the focus of the class? There is some experience with these kinds of curricula in civilization and advanced conversation courses taught at the college level. The civilization courses are organized around the learning of content about culture and civilization. Since they tend to be more advanced courses, the foreign language serves more as a tool than as the subject of instruction. If we were to imagine a lower-level culture course, in which students were learning language along with the culture, we would see that the language instruction would not be organized along grammatical lines but rather in a way that supported the central material of the course—the culture and civilization topics. Similarly, in a conversation course whose goal is to advance students from one level of speaking proficiency to the next, grammar instruction has to be coordinated with the functions and content that belong to the desired level. We hope that discussions of such alternative curricula at the high school level will be fostered by this book. We hope to see teachers in each school district considering, revising, and improving the design of their foreign language programs, trying to find the appropriate balance among grammar, communication, and culture.

The role of literature in the secondary school curriculum deserves renewed consideration. The reading of literature in general has declined in the United States, and literature courses at all levels and in all languages do not attract students in great numbers. For example, the Advanced Placement (AP) Program of the College Board offers course descriptions and examinations in French literature, in Spanish literature, and in Latin (Vergil and Catullus-Horace). The general trend of increased interest in language study as opposed to literature can be seen in candidate volumes for French and Spanish; while the number of students involved in French language and Spanish language grows annually, the number of candidates enrolled in literature courses has remained about the same for many years.

The question of what to teach at the upper levels requires careful examination in each local situation. Most advanced programs teach literature to some degree, but the amount of time that should be devoted to literature, contemporary readings, and oral and written expression can vary considerably from school to school. Local circumstances may indicate, for example, that students will have better reason to stay with foreign language study longer if advanced courses focus on practical communication and language for special purposes, such as law enforcement or health care. In other cases, students may be headed for colleges whose upper-division courses focus largely on literary history and criticism. In such cases, students will profit more from the study of literature while they are still in high school.

Perhaps the success or failure of literature in the foreign language curriculum has more to do with the changing objectives of prerequisite courses than with student abilities. As the curriculum of beginning courses has changed to focus more on oral communication and less on reading and writing, students arrive at advanced courses with preparation that may not serve them well in a traditional literature class. Teachers of literature can explore ways to capitalize on students' oral skills while working to help them increase their skills in reading for meaning, writing summaries and interpretations, using a dictionary, and so forth. The apparent tension between language and literature is an important topic for both secondary and postsecondary teachers. Resolving conflicts and achieving an appropriate balance between these two elements will require careful and constructive discussion.

Increasing the Length of the Foreign Language Sequence

Most students who study a foreign language at the secondary level stop after two years. If there is a consensus on any question among language teachers, it is that two years is not enough. More than two years are usually needed to achieve the outcomes described in the Green Book. In addition, it is almost certain that students who stop language study after only two years will retain very little of what they have learned.

School language programs in other countries are quite different from ours. Language is most often an expected and a required part of the curriculum; students begin their first foreign language by age 10 and often add a second one in high school. The sequence is continuous, and students finish preuniversity education with six or more years of language study. Questions of curriculum aside, we need to consider ways to start language study as early as possible and to retain students in language classes through their senior year.

In practice this is difficult to do. Many organizational and administrative difficulties have to be overcome. Moreover, students drop out after two or three years for a number of reasons: They may have completed the years needed to enter college, they may have schedule conflicts with other advanced courses, or they may not have developed skills or interest in the subject. Teachers can combat some of these reasons by establishing better communications with guidance counselors, other administrators, and parents. It can be suggested, for example, that while few colleges have a foreign language entrance requirement, more are considering an exit requirement. Students who have studied a language for four or more years through their senior year in high school are most likely to be prepared for the college language requirements or expectations. Some postsecondary institutions are looking closely at proficiency-based requirements. As this movement gains momentum, students who have had the longest sustained experience with another language will be best prepared to meet college requirements as well as the future demands of the workplace.

One proven way to approach guidance counselors is to supply them with answers to questions that students most often ask about foreign language. The answers may vary widely from school to school, although the questions themselves will virtually be identical. The following are representative of questions identified by Galloway in cooperation with foreign language teachers in South Carolina.[1]

1. Are foreign languages only for "good" students?
2. Will it do me any good to take a foreign language if I don't go on to college?
3. If I take a foreign language, will I be able to exempt some college courses?
4. Is it better to take four years of one language or two years of two languages?
5. Which language should I take, French or Spanish? Is one easier than the other?
6. Will studying a foreign language help me on the SAT?
7. Can I take a foreign language if I don't do well in English?

Teachers are in the best position to deal with the boredom or defeatism that causes students to drop out of language study. One common problem that affects student motivation is a lack of artic-ulation between the junior high and the senior high program. When students see that they are repeating material they have already learned or think that they do not have a way to demonstrate and build on the skills and knowledge they have already acquired, it is natural for them to be discouraged and resist taking a course that seems to be largely repetitious. Teacher discussions within a dis-trict can lead to the design of an articulated five- or six-year lan-guage program so that all students have enough time to reach the basic Green Book proficiency outcomes and work toward the ad-vanced outcomes as well.

Our focus on high school language study and, to a lesser extent, on that of the junior high school should not be taken as lack of support for beginning such study even earlier. Much has been said about how easily young children learn a foreign language, but the research does not support an across-the-board "the earlier the

---

1. Vicki B. Galloway, "Public Relations: Making an Impact," in *Action for the '80s: A Political, Professional, and Public Program for Foreign Language Edu-cation,* ed. June K. Phillips (Skokie, Illinois: National Textbook Company, 1981).

better" position. Simply placing youngsters in elementary language classes is not a magic formula for success. The success of a language program at any level is dependent on the match between program goals and the characteristics of the learners, as well as on the articulation between one stage and the next. The beginning courses for younger children must be designed to capitalize on their stage of cognitive and affective development. They cannot be as grammar-based as are most current first-year courses for high school students. On the other hand, younger learners will move on to the next stage with better pronunciation, more vocabulary, and less inhibition about communicating than their high school counterparts have, and the teachers who receive them have to be prepared with more advanced goals and activities in those areas. Discussions about early language study would best proceed on this basis.

Building Bridges: The Importance of Collaboration

This book has been written for high school teachers. But much of what we have said about language teaching applies equally well to colleagues at the college level. Foreign language teachers at all levels address many of the same goals and problems, and the differences that separate us are far fewer than the common goals and concerns that unite us.

The Educational EQuality Project's Models Program for School-College Collaboration is one effort to foster cooperation between teachers at the two levels. The foreign language profession has given rise to another project devoted to establishing and fostering school-college collaboration. Academic Alliances, based at the University of Pennsylvania under the leadership of Claire Gaudiani, has helped teachers in local groups to stay up-to-date on recent developments in the field; to study texts and concepts of central importance to foreign language; and to focus on local, regional, and national issues that are related in some way to foreign language education. Such arrangements for promoting discussion and collaboration among teachers in secondary and higher education themselves deserve wider consideration.

Interdisciplinary programs or courses are a type of "horizontal" collaboration within a school, in which students use the foreign language as a means to learn another subject. At the elementary level a small number of immersion and partial immersion programs, for the most part based on the Canadian model, teach part or all of the regular program in the second language. At the high school level some magnet schools that concentrate on foreign language teach social studies, science, and mathematics in a language other than English.

Foreign language is an ideal subject for this kind of interdisciplinary connection, since students can continue to strengthen their skills while concentrating on another subject area. Not all schools can provide opportunities of this sort to students, because the number of teachers of, say, history, art, or biology who are also proficient enough in another language to teach their subject in it is limited. Where the possibility exists, however, it should be seriously discussed, for it provides an absolutely authentic situation for foreign language learners to use their newly acquired skills.

Another sort of collaboration among teachers in a given school involves bringing together in cooperative ventures programs in foreign languages, bilingual education, and English as a Second Language (ESL). While the Spanish teacher may struggle to find authentic materials about teenagers in Spanish-speaking cultures, the ESL teacher may have five such teenagers in the classroom next door. Similarly, the texts used by the bilingual education teacher for an elementary school class of Haitian children may find a useful place as supplementary reading material for a high school French class.

Teaching native speakers is a task with challenges and rewards of its own. These students most often have well-developed oral skills but weak literacy skills, and the teacher's job is to build on students' strengths while addressing the areas in need of improvement. Teachers need different strategies for this audience and can probably learn a great deal from the experience of colleagues in the English department.

Some districts have been able to place native speakers in a separate course or track designed for them. Teaching such a course involves many considerations, especially cultural sensitivity. Those who are familiar with the discussions among English teachers about black English vernacular and its relationship to standard English forms will recognize many similarities in the current discussions of familiar and standard varieties of Spanish or French. The role of the foreign language teacher is to encourage these students to continue to develop their skills in their home language and in English, so that they can function in society as bicultural, biliterate adults.

Teacher Preparation and In-Service Training

The many recent reports on education have focused attention on the teaching profession with an intensity that has not been felt for many years. One overriding theme is the movement toward high standards and the demonstration of teacher competency. In a recent article on issues in teacher education, Wing classified three areas of competency that concern foreign language teachers: target language competencies, generic classroom teaching competencies, and specialized foreign language teaching competencies.[2]

In recent discussions of certification standards in foreign language, attention has centered on proficiency, especially oral proficiency. This is a challenge for in-service as well as future teachers, since maintaining teachers' fluency involves a serious commitment of time and financial resources. Teachers need to be proficient enough in the language so that they can easily communicate the language in context within a classroom situation. They should also be models of the language proficiency they hope their students will emulate.

The history of foreign language education has been characterized by a series of movements. What should constitute the subject matter of a foreign language program and how it should be taught continue to change. Teachers must be prepared to undertake continual learning during the whole of their professional careers, for certainly the theories and practices they learned as students will be called into question, and our understanding of the language

---

2. Barbara H. Wing, "For Teachers: A Challenge for Competence," in *The Challenge for Excellence in Foreign Language Education*, ed. Gilbert A. Jarvis (Middlebury, Vermont: Northeast Conference, 1984), pp. 11-45.

learning process will grow and change. What is most important is that teachers have opportunities to read and discuss the professional literature; observe their colleagues at work in the classroom; and experiment with new methods, materials, and activities.

We hope that this book will provide a starting point for in-service programs as well as more general discussions. It is doubtful that the questions raised in this chapter can ever be fully answered, and perhaps this is as it should be. It is in thoughtful discussion and debate among teachers that the best ideas are generated, and it is through our own commitment to intellectual growth that we can help all students strive for excellence.

Bibliography

Allen, Wendy W. "Toward Cultural Proficiency." In *Proficiency, Curriculum, Articulation: The Ties That Bind,* ed. Alice C. Omaggio. Middlebury, Vermont: Northeast Conference, 1985.

Asher, James J. *Learning Another Language through Actions: The Complete Teacher's Guidebook.* Los Gatos, California: Sky Oaks Production, 1977.

Bancroft, W. Jane. "The Lozanov Method and Its American Adaptations." *Modern Language Journal* 62, no. 4 (April 1978): 167-175.

Benseler, David P., and Renate A. Schulz. "Methodological Trends in College Foreign Language Instruction." *Modern Language Journal* 64, no. 1 (Spring 1980): 88-96.

Birckbichler, Diane W. "Communication and Beyond." In *The Language Connection: From the Classroom to the World,* ed. June K. Phillips in conjunction with ACTFL. Skokie, Illinois: National Textbook Company, 1977.

————. "The Challenge of Proficiency: Student Characteristics." In *The Challenge for Excellence in Foreign Language Education,* ed. Gilbert A. Jarvis. Middlebury, Vermont: Northeast Conference, 1984.

Bonin, Therese M., and Diane W. Birckbichler. "Real Communication through Interview and Conversation Cards." *Modern Language Journal* 59, no. 1 (Jan.-Feb. 1975): 22-25.

Bragger, Jeannette D. "The Development of Oral Proficiency." In *Proficiency, Curriculum, Articulation: The Ties That Bind,* ed. Alice C. Omaggio. Middlebury, Vermont: Northeast Conference, 1985.

Byrnes, Heidi. "Teaching toward Proficiency: The Receptive Skills." In *Proficiency, Curriculum, Articulation: The Ties That Bind,* ed. Alice C. Omaggio. Middlebury, Vermont: Northeast Conference, 1985.

Carroll, John B. "A Model of School Learning." *Teachers College Record* 64, no. 8 (May 1963): 723-733.

Christensen, Clay Ben. "Beyond the Desk." In *Building on Experience—Building for Success,* ed. June K. Phillips in conjunction with ACTFL. Skokie, Illinois: National Textbook Company, 1979.

College Board, The. *Academic Preparation for College: What Students Need to Know and Be Able to Do.* New York: College Entrance Examination Board, 1983.

Crawford-Lange, Linda M., and Dale L. Lange. "Doing the Unthinkable in the Second-Language Classroom: A Process for the Integration of

Language and Culture." In *Teaching for Proficiency, the Organizing Principle*, ed. Theodore V. Higgs. Lincolnwood, Illinois: National Textbook Company, 1984.

"Foreign Languages in Baltimore and Cincinnati." *Modern Language Journal* 68, no. 1 (Spring 1984): 27. Excerpted from *Basic Education*, 28, ii, 1983.

Galloway, Vicki B. "Public Relations: Making an Impact." In *Action for the 80s: A Political, Professional, and Public Program for Foreign Language Education*, ed. June K. Phillips. Skokie, Illinois: National Textbook Company, 1981.

————. "Teaching the 'Other' Student." In *Foreign Languages: Key Links in the Chain of Learning*, ed. Robert G. Mead, Jr. Middlebury, Vermont: Northeast Conference, 1983.

Gattegno, Caleb. *Teaching Foreign Languages in Schools: The Silent Way*. New York: Educational Solutions, 1972.

Gaudiani, Claire. *Teaching Writing in the Foreign Language Curriculum*. Language in Education: Theory and Practice, no. 43. Washington, D.C.: Center for Applied Linguistics, 1981.

Guntermann, Gail. "Purposeful Communication Practice: Developing Functional Proficiency in a Foreign Language." *Foreign Language Annals* 12, no. 3 (May 1979): 219-225.

————. "From Grammar to Authentic Communication in the Foreign Language Classroom." ACTFL Master Lecture Series. Monterey, California: Defense Language Institute, 1984.

———— and June K. Phillips. *Functional-Notional Concepts: Adapting the Foreign Language Textbook*. Language in Education: Theory and Practice, no. 44. Washington, D.C.: Center for Applied Linguistics, 1982.

Harlow, Linda L., W. Flint Smith, and Alan Garfinkel. "Student-Perceived Communication Needs: Infrastructure of the Functional/Notional Syllabus." *Foreign Language Annals* 13, no. 1 (Feb 1980): 11-22.

Heilenman, Laura K., and Isabelle Kaplan. "Proficiency in Practice: The Foreign Language Curriculum." In *Foreign Language Proficiency in the Classroom and Beyond*, ed. Charles J. James. Lincolnwood, Illinois: National Textbook Company, 1985.

Higgs, Theodore V. "Introduction: Language Teaching and the Quest for the Holy Grail." In *Teaching for Proficiency: the Organizing Principle*, ed. Theodore V. Higgs. Lincolnwood, Illinois: National Textbook Company, 1984.

Joiner, Elizabeth G., and June K. Phillips. "Merging Methods and Texts: A Pragmatic Approach." In *The Foreign Language Teacher: The Lifelong Learner*, ed. Robert G. Mead, Jr. Middlebury, Vermont: Northeast Conference, 1982.

Kelly, Louis G. *25 Centuries of Language Teaching: An Inquiry into the*

Science, Art, and Development of Language Teaching Methodology. Rowley, Massachusetts: Newbury House, 1976.

Knop, Constance K. "Notional-Functional Syllabus: From Theory to Classroom Applications." In *A Global Approach to Foreign Language Education,* ed. Maurice W. Conner. Skokie, Illinois: National Textbook Company, 1981.

Krashen, Stephen D. *Second Language Acquisition and Second Language Learning.* Oxford and New York: Pergamon Press, 1981.

―――. *Principles and Practice in Second Language Acquisition.* Oxford and New York: Pergamon Press, 1982.

Lambert, Wallace, and G. Richard Tucker. *The Bilingual Education of Children: The St. Lambert Experiment.* Rowley, Massachusetts: Newbury House, 1972.

Landry, Richard G. "A Comparison of Second Language Learners and Monolinguals on Divergent Thinking Tasks at the Elementary School Level." *Modern Language Journal* 58, nos. 1-2, (Jan.-Feb. 1974): 10-14.

Levy, Stephen L. "Teaching Multilevel Foreign Language Classes." *ERIC/CLL News Bulletin* 6:1 (1982): 1, 6-7.

Liskin-Gasparro, Judith E. "The ACTFL Proficiency Guidelines: A Historical Perspective." In *Teaching for Proficiency, the Organizing Principle,* ed. Theodore V. Higgs. Lincolnwood, Illinois: National Textbook Company, 1984.

Loew, Helene Z. "Working Together: Guidance Counselors and Foreign Language Teachers." *Foreign Language Annals* 11, no. 4 (Sept. 1978): 367-374.

Magnan, Sally Sieloff. "From Achievement toward Proficiency through Multi-Sequence Evaluation." In *Proficiency, Curriculum, Articulation: The Ties That Bind,* ed. Alice C. Omaggio. Middlebury, Vermont: Northeast Conference, 1985.

―――. "Teaching and Testing Proficiency in Writing: Skills to Transcend the Second-Language Classroom." In *Proficiency, Curriculum, Articulation: The Ties That Bind,* ed. Alice C. Omaggio. Middlebury, Vermont: Northeast Conference, 1985.

Masciantonio, Rudolph. "Tangible Benefits of the Study of Latin: A Review of Research." *Foreign Language Annals* 10, no. 4 (Sept. 1977): 375-382.

―――. "Language Arts through Latin: A Staff Development Project." *Foreign Language Annals* 16, no. 5 (Oct. 1983): 369-372.

Medley, Frank W., Jr. "Designing the Proficiency-Based Curriculum." In *Proficiency, Curriculum, Articulation: The Ties That Bind,* ed. Alice C. Omaggio. Middlebury, Vermont: Northeast Conference, 1985.

Met, Myriam, Helena Anderson, Evelyn Brega, and Nancy Rhodes. "Elementary School Foreign Language: Key Link in the Chain of Learning." In *Foreign Languages: Key Links in the Chain of Learning*, ed. Robert G. Mead, Jr. Middlebury, Vermont: Northeast Conference, 1983.

Omaggio, Alice C. *Games and Simulations in the Foreign Language Classroom.* Language in Education: Theory and Practice, no. 13. Arlington, Virginia: Center for Applied Linguistics, 1979.

———. *Helping Learners Succeed: Activities for the Foreign Language Classroom.* Language in Education: Theory and Practice, no. 36. Washington, D.C.: Center for Applied Linguistics, 1981.

———. *Proficiency-Oriented Classroom Testing.* Language in Education: Theory and Practice, no. 52. Washington, D.C.: Center for Applied Linguistics, 1983.

———. "The Proficiency-Oriented Classroom." In *Teaching for Proficiency, the Organizing Principle*, ed. Theodore V. Higgs. Lincolnwood, Illinois: National Textbook Company, 1984.

———, Anthony J. DeNapoli, Paul T. Griffith, Dora F. Kennedy, Stephen L. Levy, Gladys Lipton, and Helene Z. Loew. "Foreign Language in the Secondary School: Reconciling the Dream with the Reality." In *Foreign Languages: Key Links in the Chain of Learning*, ed. Robert G. Mead, Jr. Middlebury, Vermont: Northeast Conference, 1983.

Paulston, Christina Bratt, and Mary Newton Bruder. *From Substitution to Substance: A Handbook of Structural Pattern Drills.* Rowley, Massachusetts: Newbury House, 1975.

——— and Howard R. Selekman. "Interaction Activities in the Foreign Language Classroom, or How to Grow a Tulip-Rose." *Foreign Language Annals* 9, no. 3 (May 1976): 248-254.

Phillips, June K. "Practical Implications of Recent Research in Reading." *Foreign Language Annals* 17, no. 4 (Sept. 1984): 285-296.

President's Commission on Foreign Language and International Studies. *Strength through Wisdom: A Critique of U.S. Capability.* Washington, D.C.: U.S. Government Printing Office, 1979.

Rhodes, Nancy C., and Marguerite Ann Snow. "Foreign Language in the Elementary School: A Comparison of Achievement." *ERIC/CLL News Bulletin* 7:2 (1984): 3-5.

Rivers, Wilga M., ed. *A Practical Guide to the Teaching of French.* New York: Oxford University Press, 1975.

———. "A New Curriculum for New Purposes." *Foreign Language Annals* 18 no. 1 (1985): 37-43.

Seelye, H. Ned. *Teaching Culture: Strategies for Intercultural Communication.* Lincolnwood, Illinois: National Textbook Company, 1984.

Stern, H. H. "Toward a Multidimensional Curriculum." In *Foreign Languages: Key Links in the Chain of Learning*, ed. Robert G. Mead, Jr. Middlebury, Vermont: Northeast Conference, 1983.

———— and Jim Cummins. "Language Teaching/Learning Research: A Canadian Perspective in Status and Directions." In *Action for the 80s: A Political, Professional, and Public Program for Foreign Language Education*, ed. June K. Phillips. Skokie, Illinois: National Textbook Company, 1981.

Strasheim, Lorraine A. "The Issue: Multi-Level Classes." *Foreign Language Annals* 12 (1979): 423-425.

————. "Broadening the Middle School Curriculum through Content: Globalizing Foreign Languages." In *Action for the 80s: A Political, Professional, and Public Program for Foreign Language Education*, ed. June K. Phillips. Skokie, Illinois: National Textbook Company, 1981.

Strength through Wisdom: A Critique of U.S. Capability, a Report from the President's Commission on Foreign Language and International Studies. Washington, D.C.: U.S. Government Printing Office, 1979.

Swaffar, Janet K. "Reading Authentic Texts in a Foreign Language: A Cognitive Model." *Modern Language Journal* 69, no. 1 (1985): 15-34.

Swain, Merrill. "What Does Research Say about Immersion Education?" In *So You Want Your Child to Learn French?* Ottawa, Canada: Canadian Parents for French, 1979.

Symposium on Receptive Skills. Defense Language Institute, Presidio of Monterey, California, November 1983. *Foreign Language Annals* 17, no. 4 (Sept. 1984): 252-422.

Terrell, T. D. "The Natural Approach to Language Teaching: An Update." *Modern Language Journal* 66, no. 2 (Summer 1982): 121-132.

Titone, Renzo. *Teaching Foreign Languages: An Historical Sketch*. Washington, D.C.: Georgetown University Press, 1968.

Walz, Joel C. *Error Correction Techniques for the Foreign Language Classroom*. Language in Education: Theory and Practice, no. 50. Washington, D.C.: Center for Applied Linguistics, 1982.

Weatherford, H. Jarold. "Foreign Language Attitudes Survey: Georgia Superintendents and High School Principals." *Foreign Language Annals* 15, no. 1 (1982): 29-34.

Wing, Barbara H. "For Teachers: A Challenge for Competence." In *The Challenge for Excellence in Foreign Language Education*, ed. Gilbert A. Jarvis. Middlebury, Vermont: Northeast Conference, 1984.

————, ed. *Listening, Reading, Writing: Analysis and Application*. Middlebury, Vermont: Northeast Conference, 1986. Forthcoming.

Members of the Council on Academic Affairs, 1983-85

Peter N. Stearns, Heinz Professor of History, Carnegie-Mellon University, Pittsburgh, Pennsylvania (*Chair* 1983-85)

Dorothy S. Strong, Director of Mathematics, Chicago Public Schools, Illinois (*Vice Chair* 1983-85)

Victoria A. Arroyo, College Board Student Representative, Emory University, Atlanta, Georgia (1983-84)

Ida S. Baker, Principal, Cape Coral High School, Florida (1984-85)

Michael Anthony Brown, College Board Student Representative, University of Texas, Austin (1983-85)

Jean-Pierre Cauvin, Associate Professor of French, Department of French and Italian, University of Texas, Austin (1983-84)

Alice C. Cox, Assistant Vice President, Student Academic Services, Office of the President, University of California (1983-84, Trustee Liaison 1984-85)

Charles M. Dorn, Professor of Art and Design, Department of Creative Arts, Purdue University, West Lafayette, Indiana (1983-84)

Sidney H. Estes, Assistant Superintendent, Instructional Planning and Development, Atlanta Public Schools, Georgia (1983-85)

David B. Greene, Chairman, Division of Humanities, Wabash College, Crawfordsville, Indiana (1984-85)

Jan A. Guffin, Chairman, Department of English, North Central High School, Indianapolis, Indiana (1983-85)

John W. Kenelly, Professor of Mathematical Sciences, Clemson University, South Carolina (1983-85)

Mary E. Kesler, Assistant Headmistress, The Hockaday School, Dallas, Texas (Trustee Liaison 1983-85)

Arthur E. Levine, President, Bradford College, Massachusetts (1983-85)

Deirdre A. Ling, Vice Chancellor for University Relations and Development, University of Massachusetts, Amherst (Trustee Liaison 1983-84)

Judith A. Lozano-Loredo, Superintendent, Southside Independent School District, San Antonio, Texas (1983-84)